STUDY GUIDE

Steven Isonio
Golden West College

PSYCHOLOGY

TWELFTH EDITION

Charles G. Morris
University of Michigan

Albert A. Maisto
University of North Carolina at Charlotte

PEARSON

Prentice
Hall

Upper Saddle River, New Jersey 07458

Printed in the United States of America
10 9 8 7 6 5 4 3 2 1

ISBN 0-13-189148-0

Table of Contents

1

The Science of Psychology

Class and Text Notes

1. What is Psychology?

    A. The Fields of Psychology

    - Developmental Psychology

    - Neuroscience and Physiological Psychology

    - Experimental Psychology

    - Personality Psychology

    - Clinical and Counseling Psychology

    - Social Psychology

    - Industrial and Organization (I/O) Psychology

    B. Enduring Issues

    - Person–Situation

    - Nature-Nurture

    - Stability–Change

    - Diversity-Universality

    - Mind–Body

    C. Psychology as Science

Applying Psychology: Critical Thinking—A Fringe Benefit of Studying Psychology

2. The Growth of Psychology

    A. The "New Psychology": A Science of the Mind

       1. Wilhelm Wundt and Edward Bradford Titchener: Voluntarism Structuralism

       2. William James: Functionalism

       3. Sigmund Freud: Psychodynamic Psychology

B. Redefining Psychology: The Study of Behavior

    1. John B. Watson: Behaviorism

    2. B.F. Skinner: Behaviorism Revisited

C. Cognitive Revolution

    1. The Precursors: Gestalt Psychology and Humanistic Psychology

    2. The Rise of Cognitive Psychology

D. New Directions

    1. Evolutionary Psychology

    2. Positive Psychology

    3. Multiple Perspectives

E. Where Are the Women?

Thinking Critically: Autonomy

3. Human Diversity

A. Gender

    1. Gender Stereotypes

    2. Feminist Psychology

    3. Sexual Orientation

Thinking Critically: The Universal Male

B. Race and Ethnicity

    1. Racial and Ethnic Minorities in Psychology

Thinking Critically: Psychology and Minority Students

C. Culture

4. Research Methods in Psychology

A. Naturalistic Observation

B. Case Studies

C. Surveys

D. Correlational Research

2

E. Experimental Research

- Participants, independent variable, dependent variable, experimental group, control group, experimenter bias

F. Multimethod Research

G. Importance of Sampling

- Sample

- Random sample

- Representative sample

Summary Table: Basic Methods of Research

5. Ethics and Psychological Research

A. Ethics in Research on Humans

- Informed consent obtained from participants

B. Ethics in Research on Nonhuman Subjects

6. Careers in Psychology

A. Academic and Applied Psychology

B. Clinical Settings

On the Cutting Edge: Prescription Privileges for Clinical Psychologists

Web Investigations

www.prenhall.com/morris

Chapter 1: Exploring Arguments

Welcome to *Web Investigations* into psychology. *Web Investigations* are exercises and demonstrations found on the Morris Companion Web Site. They ll help you learn more about psychology within the dynamic and interactive environment of the World Wide Web.

After reading chapter 1, you should have an appreciation for a rich, diverse field of inquiry that has many applications. Students often find their first course in psychology to be the most challenging one in their college career as they learn about sensation, motivation, social behavior, personality, human development, and language to mention only a few of the topics covered in this text. Given the thousands of topics in psychology, an important question to ask is: What unifies psychology?

One factor that unifies psychology (and all sciences) is a commitment to reaching well-reasoned, rational conclusions. Psychologists use objective data to support their conclusions. At some point, you have probably heard non-psychologists offer conclusions on psychological topics that are not based on objective data. For example, spare the rod and spoil the child is often given as sound child-rearing advice, but it is based on a proverb, not on objective data. Psychological research may reach a different conclusion.

The skill of evaluating claims is an important one to develop both as a student of psychology, and as an individual in a society that daily bombards people with claims. The *Web Investigations* for this chapter will give you some practice in evaluating claims and arguments.

To access the Web Investigations for this and other chapters, just follow these steps:
- *Log on to the Internet and type in* <u>www.prenhall.com/morris</u>
- *Select the book cover for Morris, Psychology 11th edition. This will bring you to the front page of the Morris Companion Web Site. It is recommended that you <u>bookmark</u> this site for future assignments.*
- *The site will ask you for an access code. Your access code is printed on a card that is bound into this textbook. Open the card to get your access code, and enter it as requested by the Web site. Then follow the instructions to create your own user ID and password, which you will use to access this site from now on. Be sure to <u>write down</u> your user ID and password so you don't forget them.*
- *Once into the Morris Companion Web Site, select chapter 1 and click* **on Web Investigations** *to begin.*

Multiple Choice Pretest

This pretest will help you identify the topics in the chapter that are most difficult for you. By focusing your study time in those areas, you will see the greatest improvement.

1. Psychologists who study how people change as they grow older are called _____ psychologists.
   a. social
   b. clinical
   c. developmental
   d. organizational

2. Psychologists who see patients in the hospital are called _____.
   a. clinical psychologists
   b. educational psychologists
   c. industrial psychologists
   d. developmental psychologists

3. About half of all psychologists work in the area of
   a. personality or development.
   b. physiological or experimental.
   c. clinical or counseling.
   d. social or development.

4. The processes involved in learning, memory, sensation, perception, and cognition are investigated by _____ psychologists.
   a. organizational
   b. experimental
   c. educational
   d. social

5. Psychology is the study of behavior and _____.
   a. emotions
   b. functionalism
   c. mental processes
   d. structuralism

6. The _____ is composed of formulating a hypothesis, careful observations, gathering data, and analyzing the data.
   a. scientific method
   b. introspection method
   c. deductive method
   d. inductive method

7. All of the following are goals of psychology EXCEPT
   a. reinforcement.
   b. control.
   c. prediction.
   d. description.

8. Many studies have demonstrated that males are more physically aggressive than are females. This conclusion involves:
   a. description
   b. explanation
   c. prediction
   d. control

9. When you watch children play at a day care center to gather information about the difference in aggression between boys and girls, you are using the _____ research method.
   a. experimental
   b. case study
   c. correlational
   d. naturalistic observation

10. A research method that studies a person in-depth for some time through the use of observation, interviews, and writings is the _____ method.
   a. psychometric
   b. naturalistic observation
   c. survey
   d. case study

11. In _____ research questionnaires or interviews are administered to a selected group of people.
   a. correlational
   b. survey
   c. experimental
   d. analytical

12. People are sometimes given tests to predict their future performance in school or on the job. This entails the use of the _____ method.
   a. case
   b. longitudinal
   c. correlational
   d. cross sectional

13. The _____ research method should be used if the cause of a behavior is to be determined.
   a. experimental
   b. longitudinal
   c. correlational
   d. cross sectional

14. In an experiment to test the effects of stress on performance, the independent variable is _____.
   a. performance
   b. age of the person
   c. stress
   d. test score

15. In experiments, which group does not receive the treatment and is used for comparison?
   a. independent
   b. dependent
   c. experimental
   d. control

16. Population is to _____ as sample is to _____.
    a. whole; part
    b. research; subjects
    c. part; whole
    d. control; subjects

17. Milgram's research focused on _____.
    a. learning
    b. obedience
    c. biofeedback
    d. pain thresholds

18. The first psychology lab was opened by _____.
    a. Watson
    b. James
    c. Wundt
    d. Freud

19. Structuralism emphasizes _____.
    a. the basic units of experience and their combinations
    b. the influence of the unconscious
    c. biological principles
    d. individual difference

20. Functionalism emphasizes that _____.
    a. research should be done through objective introspection
    b. individual differences are the basis of human behavior
    c. consciousness is a continuous flow
    d. consciousness is composed of three elements

21. Freud believed that our behavior is controlled by _____.
    a. environmental stimuli
    b. mental associations
    c. Gestalt interactions
    d. unconscious desires

22. Freud believed that unresolved conflicts during developmental stages may result in
    _____.
    a. fixation
    b. limited perception
    c. distortion
    d. an inferiority complex

23. Behaviorism was founded by _____.
    a. James
    b. Watson
    c. Titchener
    d. Wundt

24. _____ psychologists are concerned with the scientific study of mental processes.
    a. Humanistic
    b. Existential
    c. Cognitive
    d. Behavioral

Answers and Explanations to Multiple Choice Pretest

1.   c.   Developmental psychology focuses on how people change as they age.

2.   a.   Clinical psychologists see patients in the hospital and private clinics.

3.   c.   50 percent of all psychologists work in the areas of clinical and counseling psychology.

4.   b.   Experimental psychologists study our perceptions, behaviors, and emotions.

5.   c.   The field of psychology studies behavior and mental processes.

6.   a.   The scientific method provides an excellent way to obtain and analyze data.

7.   a.   Goals of psychology are to describe, predict, and control behavior.

8.   a.   The sex difference in physical aggression is merely being described

9.   d.   Naturalistic observation involves observing a person's or an animal's behavior without interfering.

10.   d.   In the case study method a person is studied in great depth.

11.   b.   The survey method can utilize either questionnaires or face-to-face interviews.

12.   c.   Correlational studies can sometimes predict the likelihood of future outcomes.

13.   a.   Experimental method is able to show cause and effect.

14.   c.   Stress is the independent variable.

15.   d.   The control group is important for comparison to the experimental group.

16.   a.   Analogy: population is the whole group of people of interest, and the sample is a small part of the population.

17.   b.   Milgram studied obedience.

18.   c.   Wundt opened the first psychology lab.

19.   a.   Structuralism emphasizes basic units of experience and their combinations.

20.   c.   Functionalism emphasizes that consciousness is a continuous flow.

21.   d.   Freud believed our unconscious thoughts were very important.

22.   a.   Freud believed that unresolved conflict resulted in fixation at a specific psychosexual stage.

23.   b.   Watson founded behaviorism.

24.   c.   Cognitive psychologists emphasize mental processes.

Learning Objectives

After you have read and studied this chapter, you should be able to complete the following statements. Your exam is written based on these learning objectives such as these.

1. Describe the major fields of psychology including developmental, physiological, experimental, personality, clinical and counseling, social, and industrial/organization psychology.

2. Summarize the five enduring issues of psychology.

3. Distinguish between the five basic methods used by psychologists to gather information about behavior. Identify the situations in which each of the methods would be appropriate.

4. Describe the importance of sampling related to issues of gender, race, and culture in research.

5. Discuss ethical concerns related to psychological research.

6. Describe the early schools of psychology and explain how they contributed to its development.

7. Explain the difference between psychiatrists, psychologists, and psychoanalysts.

8. Describe some career options in psychology.

Short Essay Questions

Write out your answers to the following eight essay questions to further your mastery of the topics.

1. Explain what case studies are and how they are useful. What are the major advantages and disadvantages of this type of research?

_____

_____

_____

_____

_____

_____

_____

_____

_____

_____

_____

2. Discuss samples and populations. What can a researcher do to overcome obstacles to obtaining a good sample?

_____

_____

_____

_____

_____

_____

_____

_____

_____

3. Describe the correlational research method. What are the advantages and disadvantages of this type of research?

_____

_____

_____

_____

_____

_____

_____

_____

_____

_____

4. Describe Milgram's research and explain why it has been so controversial.

_____

_____

_____

_____

_____

_____

_____

_____

_____

_____

5. Explain the concept of informed consent. What are some of its components?

_____

_____

_____

_____

_____

_____

_____

_____

_____

_____

6. Describe the differences between the structuralist and functionalist schools of psychology.

_____

_____

_____

_____

_____

_____

_____

_____

_____

_____

7. Compare and contrast behaviorism and cognitive psychology.

_____

_____

_____

_____

_____

_____

_____

_____

_____

_____

8. Outline some of the key aspects of Freud's psychoanalytic theory.

_____

_____

_____

_____

_____

_____

_____

_____

_____

_____

_____

Language Support

Students identified the following words from the text as needing more explanation. This page can be cut-out, folded in half, and used as a bookmark for this chapter.

A

adherents of	those who believe in
adjacent	next to
aesthetics	what is important or beautiful
against all odds	surprisingly winning over big difficulties
agony	terrible pain
ailments	illnesses
alienation	feeling left out
all-encompassing	large, complete
apathy	not interested, bored
assimilated	included and accepting
astrology	study of the influence of the planets on humans

B

"blank slate"	unmarked surface
blunder	mistake
breadth	wide range
brutality	physical abuse
bursting into tears	start crying

C

capacity	ability, being able to
chiefly	mainly
colleagues	people you work with
collaboration	working together
commingled	mixed together racially

conduct	do
contend	believe, say
contradict	say something that doesn't agree
cultural constraints	traditions of behavior in a group

D

decorum	good behavior
despite	although it has
destiny	the direction of his life
"devil's advocate"	pretend to be against some idea
devote	spend
dissimilar	not alike
distinct	different
distinguishes	makes different
dominated	was the strongest
drawback	weakness

E

emerge	come out, show
emphasis	seen as most important
empower	makes them feel strong
encounter	find
enduring issues	things of interest for a long time
enhancing	making stronger or better
establishing himself	getting settled, doing well
evolved	developed
exchange ideas	discuss thoughts on their subject
expanding	growing
expelled	forced out
extent to	how much

F

fascinated	very interested
faulty generalization	deciding too soon, deciding without all the facts
fiancée	the person you are engaged to
firmly fixed	not easily changed
formulating	deciding
fundamental	starting

G

ghetto	slum, poor neighborhood
grasp	understand

H

harassment	bother, pestering
hybrid	combination, mix

I

impartial	not having a personal interest
improvise	make up, invent
incident	something that happens
influential	important
inhumane	cruel
impulsive	done without much thinking
interceded	helped
investigate	examine
Ivy League	a really good college

L

liaisons	partners
loopholes	mistakes

M

magna cum laude	with high honors

mechanisms	ways
"mean streets"	bad neighborhood
"miracle cure"	very helpful medical discovery
monopolize	control
mood swings	sudden changes in feelings
mutual	shared

O

obsolete	no longer needed or useful
occur	happen
offspring	children
on rotations	doing shift work
opponents	those who are against it
optimists	cheerful, happy people
orthodox	usual, traditional
over request	ask for too much
overwhelmingly	almost all

P

pecking at	tapping with beak
penchants	the things someone prefers
pessimists	people who expect the worst
phenomenon	event, occurrence
practitioners	people who put psychology into practice
precursors	what comes before
prenatal period	the time before the baby is born
prestigious	respected
prevalent	common
prohibitions	things that are not allowed
proximity	closeness

R

realm	area
recollections	memories
reluctantly	did not really want to
reassigned	sent to
repertoire	list of interests
resurface later	come out at another time
revolution	something new develops or rises up

S

scrutiny	a very close look, examine
sharper	more clear
sheds light on	helps us understand
stuttered	had difficulty speaking
subliminal	below level of senses, hidden
suckled	nursed, took care of
supplant	put instead of
suspicion	without trust
systematically	done with care, orderly

T

testosterone	hormone found more in males than females

U

universal	applies to everyone

V

variety	many types
virtually	almost, nearly

Multiple Choice Posttest

After studying the text and completing the Study Guide activities, answer these questions to determine if you need to review any areas before the course exam.

1. The problem with the straightforward definition of psychology as the science of behavior and mental processes is:
   a. it is simply incorrect
   b. it understates the depth and breadth of psychology
   c. psychologists study behavior but not mental processes
   d. it is outdated

2. Researchers have found that schizophrenia is related to excesses of dopamine chemical in the brain. These researchers would likely be _____ psychologists.
   a. clinical
   b. psychoanalytical
   c. developmental
   d. physiological

3. If you were a psychologist with research interests in basic psychological processes such as learning and motivation, you would most likely refer to yourself as a(n):
   a. clinical psychologist
   b. experimental psychologist
   c. personality psychologist
   d. educational psychologist

4. _____ psychologists work to improve efficiency of people in business.
   a. Cognitive
   b. Developmental
   c. Industrial/organizational
   d. Physiological

5. Susan is a cross-cultural psychologist who believes that many findings from psychological research on U.S. college students cannot be appropriately applied to people in other societies. She has taken a definite position on which enduring issue in psychology?
   a. person-situation
   b. nature-nurture
   c. stability-change
   d. diversity-universality

6. William James argued that consciousness is _____, whereas Titchener viewed it as _____.
   a. active; static
   b. elemental; holistic
   c. static; integrated
   d. integrated; separate

7. When studying a particular behavior, a psychologist first _____ it.
   a. describes
   b. explains
   c. controls
   d. predicts

8. A hypothesis is _____.
   a. the independent variable
   b. an explanation of a phenomenon
   c. a testable prediction derived from a theory
   d. the dependent variable

9. Research which observed behavior in its actual setting without controlling anything is called _____.
   a. correlational method
   b. naturalistic observation
   c. survey research
   d. psychometric study

10. The research method used by Freud was _____.
    a. correlational method
    b. naturalistic observation
    c. survey research
    d. case study method

11. All of the following statements are true of Freud's psychodynamic theory, except:
    a, viewed freewill is largely an illusion
    b. held that repressed unconscious impulses can affect conscious thoughts and behaviors
    c. was rather narrow in scope, focusing almost exclusively on clinical issues
       emphasized the importance of sexuality

12. The amount of association between two or more variables is _____.
    a. correlation
    b. naturalistic observation
    c. reliability
    d. synchronosity

13. The only research method that can demonstrate a cause and effect relationship between variables is the _____ method.
    a. correlational
    b. naturalistic observation
    c. survey research
    d. experimental

14. In an experiment, the researcher manipulates the _____ variable.
    a. placebo
    b. independent
    c. dependent
    d. correlational

15. Expectations by the experimenter that may have an effect on the results of an experiment are called _____.
    a. sample bias
    b. double-blind
    c. experimenter bias
    d. treatment bias

16. Population is to sample as _____ is to part.
    a. placebo
    b. independent variable
    c. dependent variable
    d. whole

17. It is important that a sample be _____ of the population.
    a.   controlled
    b.   biased
    c.   representative
    d.   independent

18. Subjects in Milgram's studies were TOLD they were taking part in studies on _____.
    a.   obedience
    b.   emotional deprivation
    c.   public humiliation
    d.   learning

19. Wundt learned to do _____.
    a.   free association
    b.   objective introspection
    c.   subjective introspection
    d.   psychoanalysis

20. The basic units of experience and their combinations were the foundation of _____.
    a.   functionalism
    b.   structuralism
    c.   Gestalt
    d.   behaviorism

21. Consciousness as a continuous flow is an important concept to _____.
    a.   structuralism
    b.   functionalism
    c.   objective introspection
    d.   behaviorism

22. Freud believed that adult problems usually _____.
    a.   result in Freudian slips
    b.   result in bad dreams
    c.   can be traced back to critical stages during childhood
    d.   are the result of poor behaviors

23. _____ believed that a child must overcome a sense of inferiority.
    a.   Adler
    b.   Freud
    c.   Jung
    d.   Maslow

24. Gestalt theory emphasizes _____.
    a.   a flow of consciousness
    b.   the atoms of thought
    c.   environmental stimuli
    d.   our tendency to see patterns

25. What did B. F. Skinner mean when he referred to the mind as a "black box"?
    a.   conditioning is difficult to understand
    b.   very little light enters the cranium through the ears
    c.   psychologists should be concerned only about what goes into the "black box" and what comes out, not what goes on inside
    d.   previous attempts to understand the mind had failed miserably

Answers and Explanations to Multiple Choice Posttest

1.   b.   Contemporary psychology is a very broad and diverse field.

2.   d.   Physiological psychology studies the chemistry of the brain.

3.   b.   Experimental psychologists study processes such as learning and motivation.

4.   c.   Industrial/organization psychology work to make businesses more efficient.

5.   d.   The diversity/universality issue includes questions about the applicability of research findings to a wide range of cultures.

6.   a.   James viewed consciousness as active; Titchner saw it as static.

7.   a.   The first goal of psychology is to describe behavior.

8.   c.   A hypothesis is a testable prediction.

9.   b.   Naturalistic observation involves watching a research subject in the natural setting.

10.   d.   Freud's research and theory were build upon case studies.

11.   c.   Freud's theory is very broad in scope, and all-encompassing.

12.   a.   Correlational research can determine the amount of association between variables.

13.   d.   Only the experimental method can show cause and effect.

14.   b.   A researcher manipulates the independent variable.

15.   c.   Experimenter bias can be caused by the expectations of the researcher.

16.   d.   Analogy: Population is to sample as whole is to part.

17.   c.   A sample is representative of the population when it contains the same proportion of various diverse groups.

18.   d.   Milgram subjects were told the research was about learning, but this was not true.

19.   b.   Wundt learned to do objective introspection.

20.   b.   Structuralism focuses on basic units of experiences and their combinations.

21.   b.   Consciousness as a continuous flow is important to functionalism.

22.   c.   Freud believed that a child's first five years are critically important to adult development.

23.   a.   Adler believed a child must overcome a sense of inferiority to develop normally.

24.   d.   Gestalt theory emphasizes our tendency to see patterns.

25.   c.   As a behaviorist, Skinner was interested in stimuli and behavior, not thoughts.

2

The Biological Basis of Behavior

Class and Text Notes

1. Neurons: The Messengers

    A. Cell Body

    B. Dendrites

    C. Axon

    D. Myelin sheath

    E. Sensory (or afferent) Neurons

    F. Motor (or efferent) Neurons

    G. Interneurons (or association neurons)

    H. Glial Cells (or glia)

2. The Neural Impulse

    A. Ions

    B. Resting Potential

    C. Polarization/Depolarization

    D. Neural Impulse (Action Potential)

    E. Graded Potential

    F. Threshold of Excitation

    G. All-or-None Law

    H. Absolute Refractory Period

    I. Relative Refractory Period

3. The Synapse

    A. Synaptic Space (synaptic cleft)

    B. Terminal Button (synaptic knob)

    C. Synapse

D. Synaptic Vesicles

E. Neurotransmitters

F. Receptor Sites

4. Neurotransmitters

5. Psychopharmacology

Enduring Issues: Neural Plasticity

6. Neural Plasticity and Neurogenesis

Applying Psychology: Can the Brain and Nervous System Repair Themselves?

7. The Central Nervous System

    A. The Organization of the Nervous System

    B. The Brain

       • The Central Core

          – Hindbrain

          – Cerebellum

          – Midbrain

          – Thalamus

          – Hypothalamus

          – Reticular Formation (RF)

       • Limbic System

       • Cerebral Cortex

          – Association areas

          – Occipital Lobe

          – Temporal Lobe

          – Parietal Lobe

          – Primary Somatosensory Cortex

          – Frontal Lobe

          – Primary Motor Cortex

8. Hemispheric Specialization

A.   Corpus Callosum

Thinking Critically: Einstein's Brain

B.   Language

9.   Tools for Studying the Brain

   A.   Microelectrode Techniques

   B.   Macroelectrode Techniques

   C.   Structural Imaging

   •   Computerized Axial Tomography (CT-scan)

   •   Magnetic Resonance Imaging (MRI)

   D.   Functional Imaging

   •   EEG

   •   Magnetoencephalography (MEG)

   •   Magnetic Source Imagining (MSI)

   •   Positron Emission Tomography (PET)

   •   Radioactive PET

   •   Single Photon Emission Computed Tomography (SPECT)

   •   Functional magnetic resonance imaging (fMRI)

10.   Spinal Cord

11.   The Peripheral Nervous System

   A.   The Somatic Nervous System

   B.   The Autonomic Nervous System

   •   Sympathetic Division

   •   Parasympathetic Division

12.   The Endocrine System

   A.   Hormones

   B.   The Thyroid Gland

   C.   The Parathyroid Glands

   D.   The Pineal Gland

E. The Pancreas

F. The Pituitary Gland

G. The Gonads

H. The Adrenal Glands

13. Genes, Evolution, and Behavior

Enduring Issues: Nature Nurture-The Pendulum Swings

A. Genetics

- Genes

- Chromosomes

- Deoxyribonucleic Acid (DNA)

- Human genome

- Dominant gene; Recessive gene

- Polygenic inheritance

B. Behavior Genetics

- Animal Behavior Genetics

    – Strain studies

    – Selection Studies

- Human Behavior Genetics

    – Family Studies

    – Twin Studies

    – Adoption Studies

    – Molecular Genetics

On the Cutting Edge: In Search of the Human Genome

C. Evolutionary Psychology

- Natural Selection

On the Cutting Edge: Engineering Smarter Mice

Thinking Critically: Depression

D.   Social Implications

Thinking Critically: Media Accounts of Research

Web Investigations
www.prenhall.com/morris

Chapter 2: Action at the Synapse

The synapse, or the structures responsible for interneural communication, is an important element in our understanding of the operation of the entire nervous system. As we noted in this chapter, many *psychoactive substances* ("chemical substances that change moods and perceptions") have the effects that they do because they alter the processes at the synapse. Some, such as the paralytic curare, block receptor sites such that the neurotransmitter (acetylcholine in this case) cannot affect a nerve impulse in the receiving cell. Others may mimic a neurotransmitter, as tetrahydrocannabinal seems to mimic the neurotransmitter anandamide.

Understanding how synaptic processes operate, then, is the key to appreciating the complex neurochemical processes underlying neuronal intercommunication. This *Web Investigation* will describe these processes in additional detail.

To begin, go to the Morris Companion Web Site at the internet address shown above, select chapter 2, and click on **Web Investigations**. Give your brain a workout as you learn more about biological aspects of behavior.

Multiple Choice Pretest

This pretest will help you identify the topics in the chapter that are most difficult for you. By focusing your study time in those areas, you will see the greatest improvement.

1. A single long fiber extending from the cell body that carries outgoing messages is called a/an
   a. dendrite.   c. nerve.
   b. axon.   d. terminal.

2. All of the following are types of neurons, *except*:
   a. sensory (afferent)
   b. interneurons (association)
   c. glia (nonferent)
   d. motor (or efferent)

3. Neurons speak a language that can be characterized as:
   a. audible to powerful listening devices
   b. similar to English, but entailing richer imagery
   c. similar to the flow of electricity within circuits
   d. simple yes-no, on-off electrochemical impulses

4. The primary purpose of the myelin sheath is to _____.
   a. provide a covering for the axon
   b. receive messages from outside the neuron and carry them to the cell nucleus
   c. insulate the neuron so the action potential is faster
   d. regulate neural respiration

5. Information flow within a single neuron moves from structure to structure in which sequence:
   a. dendrites, axon, terminal button
   b. dendrites, synaptic knob, axon
   c. synaptic knob, axon, terminal button
   d. synaptic knob, dendrites, axon

6. Electrically charged particles are called _____.
   a. neurotransmitters   c. inhibitors
   b. electroparticles   d. ions

7. The time period after a neural impulse when the neuron cannot fire again is called the
   a. relative refractory period.
   b. absolute refractory period.
   c. neural action potential.
   d. ionization state.

8. When the electrical charge inside a neuron is negative in relation to the outside, the neuron is said to be in a state of _____.
   a. depolarization   c. equilibrium
   b. polarization   d. shock

9. The _____ is composed of the axon terminal, the synaptic space, and the dendrite of the next neuron.
   a. synapse   c. reception
   b. vesicle   d. transmitter site

10. _____ is the chemical substance which is involved in the reduction of pain.
   a. Myelin   c. Norepinephrine
   b. Hormones   d. Endorphin

11. Breathing, heart rate, and blood pressure are controlled by the _____.
   a. medulla   c. hypothalamus
   b. limbic system   d. cerebral cortex

12. Analysis and problem solving are handled in the _____.
   a. thalamus   c. cerebral cortex
   b. hypothalamus   d. corpus callosum

13. What structure connects the two hemispheres of the brain and coordinates their activities?
   a. reticular formation   c. hippocampus
   b. amygdala   d. corpus callosum

14. The occipital lobe receives and interprets _____ information.
   a. auditory   c. visual
   b. pain   d. bodily position

15. The main function of the _____ is to alert and arouse the higher parts of the brain.
   a. limbic system   c. amygdala
   b. reticular formation d. hippocampus

16. An injury to the _____ results in difficulty maintaining balance and coordinating movements.
   a. cerebellum   c. cerebral cortex
   b. medulla   d. hypothalamus

17. The rate of metabolism is controlled by the hormone _____.
   a. insulin   c. glycogens
   b. thyroxin   d. estrogen

18. Which is activated in an emergency?
   a. somatic nervous system
   b. sympathetic division of the autonomic nervous system
   c. peripheral nervous system
   d. parasympathetic division of the autonomic nervous system

19. The _____ regulates the stress response and is involved with emotional behavior.
   a. hypothalamus   c. cerebellum
   b. amygdala   d. medulla

20. The part of the brain that helps us focus on one thing and ignore distractions is the
   a. endocrine system.   c. parietal lobe.
   b. reticular formation. d. temporal lobe.

21. _____ studies are used to examine the relative influence on behavior of heredity and the environment.
   a. Newton   c. Twin
   b. Strain   d. Stress

22. Behavior genetics is most concerned with
   a. studying the process of natural selection.
   b. controlling behavior through genetic manipulation.
   c. determining the influence of heredity on behavior.
   d. understanding how the environment can affect phenotype.

23. For many characteristics several genes work together in a process called _____.
    a. genetic dominance
    b. behavioral genetics
    c. natural selection
    d. polygenic inheritance

24. Which of the following have the most similar genetic composition?
    a. fraternal twins   c. identical twins
    b. siblings   d. cousins

25. Activity levels of the brain are examined using _____.
    a. PET-scans   c. CT-scans
    b. NMR   d. X-ray

26. All of the following show structure EXCEPT
    a. PET-scans.   c. CT-scans.
    b. NMR.   d. X-ray.

27. The brain scanning technique that allows researchers to compare the brain activity of normal learners to that of children with learning problems, such as ADHD, is _____.
    a. PET-scans   c. CT-scans
    b. EEG   d. fMRI

28. Rhythmic variations in electrical activity are generated when a large number of neurons fire in the brain. These variations are called _____.
    a. oscillations   c. biorhythms
    b. neural impulses   d. brain waves

29. Which endocrine structure produces the largest number of different hormones and thus has the widest range of effects on the body?
    a. pancreas
    b. pituitary gland
    c. gonads
    d. thyroid gland

Answers and Explanations to Multiple Choice Pretest

1.   b.   The axon is a long fiber extending from the cells body that carries outgoing messages.

2.   c.   Glia cells are not a type of neuron.

3.   c.   The myelin sheath insulates the axon and allows the neural impulse to "jump" and travel more quickly.

4.   d.   Neurons speak in a language of simple yes-no, on-off electrochemical impulses.

5.   a.   Information flow within a neuron is from dendrites, to axon, and then to terminal button.

6.   d.   Ions are positive or negative particles.

7.   b.   Neurons cannot fire during the absolute refractory period.

8.   b.   Polarization results when the electrical charge is different on the two sides of a membrane.

9.   a.   The axon terminal, the synaptic space, and the dendrite of the next neuron make up the synapse.

10.   d.   Endorphins are involved in the reduction of pain.

11.   a.   Breathing, heart rate, and blood pressure are controlled by the medulla.

12.   c.   Analysis and problem solving are handled in the cerebral cortex.

13.   d.   The corpus callosum connects the two hemispheres and coordinates their activities.

14.   c.   Visual information is process in occipital lobe.

15.   b.   The reticular formation arouses the brain.

16.   a.   The cerebellum coordinates movements and maintains balance.

17.   b.   Metabolism is controlled by thyroxin.

18.   b.   The sympathetic nervous system is active in an emergency.

19.   a.   The hypothalamus regulates the stress response and emotional behavior.

20.   b.   Reticular formation helps us to focus.

21.   c.   Twin studies are used to examine the influence of heredity and the environment on behavior.

22.   c.   Behavior genetics is most concerned with determining the influence of heredity on behavior.

23.   d.   Genes work together in a process called polygenic inheritance.

24.   c.   Identical twins are thought to have the most similar genetic information of any relative.

25.   a.   The PET-scan examines activity of the brain.

26.   a.   CT-scans, NMR, and X-Ray all show structure.

27. d. fMRI allows researchers to compare brain activity in normal learners versus those with learning problems.

28. d. Brain waves are rhythmic variations in electrical activity.

29. b. The pituitary gland has gland produces the greatest variety of hormones and has the widest ranging effects compared with endocrine structures.

Learning Objectives

After you have read and studied this chapter, you should be able to complete the following statements. Your exam is written based on these learning objectives.

1.   Describe the structure of neurons. Trace the path of a neural impulse and explain how it transmits messages from cell to cell.

2.   Explain how neurons communicate. Identify the role of neurotransmitters and receptor. Describe the effect of drugs on the synapse.

3.   Describe the divisions and structures of the brain and explain the roles of each.

4.   Identify the functions of the sensory and motor projection areas. Describe the abilities of the two hemispheres of the cerebral cortex.

5.   Describe the structure of and function of the reticular formation, limbic, system, and spinal cord.

6.   Identify the division of the peripheral nervous system and the autonomic nervous system and explain how they work together to regulate the glands and smooth muscles of the body.

7.   Describe the functions of the endocrine system. Explain how hormones released by the endocrine system affect metabolism, blood-sugar level, sex characteristics, and the body's reaction to stress.

8.   Summarize the concerns of behavior genetics.

9.   Describe the structure of chromosomes and the role they play in inherited traits and characteristics.

10.   Explain the concepts of dominant and recessive genes.

11.   Identify several approaches to studying heritability of a trait.

12.   Discuss some social implications of behavior genetics.

Short Essay Questions

Write out your answers to the following essay questions to further your mastery of the topics.

1. Explain how an action potential occurs and how a neuron returns to the resting state.

_____

_____

_____

_____

_____

_____

_____

_____

_____

_____

2. Explain how caffeine and cocaine impact neural communication and human behavior.

_____

_____

_____

_____

_____

_____

_____

_____

_____

_____

3. Compare and contrast the functions of the left and right hemispheres of the cerebral cortex.

_____

_____

_____

_____

_____

_____

_____

_____

_____

_____

4. How do twin studies provide insights into environmental and genetic influences?

_____

_____

_____

_____

_____

_____

_____

_____

_____

_____

5.   Describe the functions of the medulla, cerebellum, thalamus, hypothalamus, and cerebral cortex.

_____

_____

_____

_____

_____

_____

_____

_____

_____

_____

6.   Compare the functions of the sympathetic and parasympathetic nervous system.

_____

_____

_____

_____

_____

_____

_____

_____

_____

_____

_____

_____

7. Describe the functions of the frontal lobes, occipital lobes, temporal lobes, and parietal lobes.

_____

_____

_____

_____

_____

_____

_____

_____

_____

_____

_____

8. Can the brain and nervous system repair themselves? Briefly summarize recent research findings.

_____

_____

_____

_____

_____

_____

_____

_____

_____

_____

_____

_____

_____

Language Support

Students identified the following words from the text as needing more explanation. This page can be cut out, folded in half, and used as a bookmark for this chapter.

A

accumulate	collect
alter	change
anthropology	study of other times and cultures
apparently	seems to be
artificial	not natural
ascending	going up
assumption	what we suppose
astonished	very surprised
attention deficits	not able to concentrate
attract	get someone to like you

B

bizarre	very weird
bundled	grouped
burrows	holes where small animals live

C

cadavers	dead human bodies
capacity	ability to do something
comprehension	understanding
compressed	made shorter
concentrated	located
considerable accuracy	reasonably exact
continuous	without stops
coordinate	put in order
crave	want very badly

D

descending	going down
delayed onset	beginning later
deleterious	bad
detach	separate from
detecting	finding
dexterity	control of movements
disrupting	stopping for a while
distinguish	tell or see differences
distinguished	told apart, differences seen
diverse	different, distant
dominant	strongest
double helix	two swirls, like twisted wire

E

ebullient	lively
elicit	bring out, cause to happen
embedded	placed within
enabling	allowing, helping
encounters	meetings
environment	outside world
equivalent	the same
exhibited	shown
exist	are there

F

| facet | part |
| facilitate | to bring about or encourage |

H

| heighten | make more intense, make feelings stronger |

I

implies	suggests
inaugurated	started
inbred	mated with close relatives
index	measure or sign of something
insulates	protects by covering
integrate	bring together
interpret	decide on meaning
intricate	complicated
intriguing	interesting
investigating	looking at, studying

J

jerky	clumsy, sudden movements
leapfrog	jump from one point to another

L

LSD "trip"	strange visual effects of drug taking

M

merges	blends, joins
miraculously	very surprisingly
morphine	pain-relieving drug

O

operates	works
opposite effects	different results
overwhelmed	shocked

P

paralysis	inability to move
performs	carries out, does
perpetuating	keeping going

physician	medical doctor
pioneered	started
plasticity	ability to change
pours	sends
prevalent	common, usual
primitive vertebrates	animals with simple body structure
prolonged	kept going
promising	hopeful
provocation	irritation, annoyance

R

| recycled | used again |
| reveals | shows |

S

sequentially	in order of time
shallow	not deep, not serious
shed light on	help us understand
spark	like a flash of lightning
sparked much controversy	been argued about a lot
spasms	jumpy movements
stamina	ability to stay active for a long time without rest
subdued	controlled, made less
susceptibility	likely to
sustain	keep going

T

tamping iron	pole
temperament	a person's nature, character
tendency	thing that makes people likely to
three-dimensional	not flat, looks like real-life

U

underlie	are the reason for
underside	lowest part
unjust	unfair

V

vice versa	opposite arrangement is also true
virtually	almost

W

wanders	walks slowly aimlessly
widespread effects	many different ways of affecting (changing)

Multiple Choice Posttest

After studying the text and completing the Study Guide activities, answer these questions to determine if you need to review any areas before the course exam.

1. Short fibers that branch out from the cell body and pick up incoming messages are called
   a. dendrites.
   b. axons.
   c. nerves.
   d. terminals.

2. The metabolism of the neuron occurs in the _____.
   a. dendrites.
   b. axons.
   c. nerves.
   d. cell body.

3. Neurons that receive information from sensory organs and relay that information to the spinal cord and the brain are called _____.
   a. association neurons
   b. efferent neurons
   c. afferent neurons
   d. ions

4. When a neuron is polarized, _____.
   a. potassium ions pass freely through the cell membrane
   b. the electrical charge inside is positive relative to the outside
   c. it cannot fire
   d. the electrical charge inside is negative relative to the outside

5. If the stimulation of a neuron causes only a subthreshold change in electrical charge, the result is called _____.
   a. a graded potential
   b. an action potential
   c. diffusion
   d. a refraction

6. The "all or none" law refers to _____.
   a. a group of neurons firing together
   b. a neuron fires at full strength or not at all
   c. all the dendrites must be receiving messages telling the neuron to fire or it will not fire at all
   d. all the neurons in a single nerve fire simultaneously

7. A person with Parkinson's disease probably has a deficiency of _____.
   a. norepinephrine
   b. serotonin
   c. dopamine
   d. acetylcholine

8. Morphine and other opiates are able to bind to the receptor sites for _____.
   a. acetylcholine
   b. hypothalamus
   c. dopamine
   d. endorphins

9. Eating, drinking, sexual behavior, sleeping and temperature control are regulated by the _____.
   a. thalamus
   b. hypothalamus
   c. cerebral cortex
   d. corpus callosum

10. What structure connects the two hemispheres of the brain and coordinates their activities?
    a. reticular formation
    b. amygdala
    c. hippocampus
    d. corpus callosum

11. A split-brain patient stares at a spot on a projection screen. A picture of a baseball is projected to the right side of the spot, and a hammer is projected to the left. What is his response when asked to say what he sees?
    a. He reports seeing an elongated baseball
    b. He says he sees a baseball
    c. He says he can't see anything besides the spot in the center of the screen
    d. He says he sees a hammer

12. Which match between structure and function is *not* correct?
    a. occipital lobe – receives and processes visual information
    b. cerebellum – coordinates movement and balance
    c. thalamus – major sensory relay center
    d. amygdala – visual spatial abilities

13. The temporal lobe receives and interprets _____ information.
    a. auditory   c. visual
    b. pain   d. bodily position

14. A part of the brain that sends the signal "Alert" to higher centers of the brain in response to incoming messages is _____.
    a. limbic system   c. amygdala
    b. reticular formation d. hippocampus

15. An injury to the _____ results in difficulty with memory.
    a. cerebellum   c. cerebral cortex
    b. medulla   d. hippocampus

16. The thyroid gland controls _____.
    a. glucose absorption c. metabolism
    b. emotions   d. sexuality

17. A car almost hit you as you were walking across the street. Which nervous system did this event probably activate in you?
    a. somatic   c. peripheral
    b. sympathetic   d. parasympathetic

18. Which hemisphere of the cerebral cortex is usually dominant in spatial tasks?
    a. frontal   c. lateral
    b. left   d. right

19. The limbic system is responsible for _____.
    a. controlling learning and emotional behavior
    b. providing a bridge for numerous brain areas
    c. analyzing problems situations
    d. fighting pathogens

20. Reflexes are usually controlled by the _____.
    a. frontal lobe   c. spinal cord
    b. medulla   d. hypothalamus

21. A person's genetic information is carried by
    a. acetylcholine   c. DNA
    b. thyroxin   d. NMR

22. _____ is a test on a fetus to determine if there are any genetic abnormalities.
    a. Amniocentesis
    b. Positron emission tomography
    c. Magnetic resonance
    d. CT-scans

23. What are the social implications of amniocentesis when abnormalities are found?
    a. Should society protect the unborn baby?
    b. Does a child with genetic abnormalities have a right to life?
    c. Are any defects are so unacceptable that abortion is justified?
    d. All of the above are social considerations.

24. What technique would you use to determine if someone is having difficulty processing visual information?
    a. PET-scans   c. CT-scans
    b. NMR   d. X-ray

25. All of the following show activity EXCEPT
    a. PET.   c. EEG.
    b. MRI.   d. MEG.

26. The gonads produce the male sex hormones called _____.
    a. oxytocin   c. progesterone
    b. thyroxin   d. testosterone

Answers and Explanations to Multiple Choice Posttest

1.   a.   Dendrites branch out from the cell body and pick up incoming messages.

2.   d.   The metabolism of the neuron occurs in the cell body.

3.   c.   Afferent neurons receive information from sensory organs and are called sensory neurons.

4.   d.   Polarization is the result of unequal distribution of charged molecules across the membrane.

5.   a.   A graded potential is a change in polarization that is not large enough to reach threshold.

6.   b.   "All of none" refers to the principle that a neuron either fires at full strength or not at all.

7.   c.   A person with Parkinson's disease probably has a deficiency of dopamine.

8.   d.   Morphine can bind to the receptor sites for endorphins.

9.   b.   The hypothalamus regulates eating, drinking, sexual behavior, sleeping, and temperature.

10.   d.   The corpus callosum connects the two hemispheres of the brain.

11.   b.   He reports seeing a baseball, because images of objects to the right of the midpoint are projected to the left (verbal) hemisphere.

12.   d.   The amygdala governs emotions related to self-preservation, not visual/spatial abilities.

13.   a.   The temporal lobe receives auditory information.

14.   b.   The reticular formation gives the "alert" signal.

15.   d.   The hippocampus is important to memory.

16.   c.   The thyroid gland controls metabolism.

17.   b.   The sympathetic nervous system is activated when we experience fear.

18.   d.   Spatial tasks are usually handled in the right hemisphere.

19.   a.   The limbic system is responsible for controlling learning and emotional behavior.

20.   c.   The spinal cord controls most reflexes.

21.   c.   DNA contains our genetic information.

22.   a.   Amniocentesis involves extracting and examining genetic information.

23.   d.   All of the statements are considerations.

24.   a.   Only PET scans look at activity levels that would take place during processing.

25.   b.   MRI shows structure only.

26.   d.   Testosterone is the male hormone produced by the gonads.

3

Sensation and Perception

CLASS AND TEXT NOTES

Sensation   -   The experience of sensory stimulation

Perception   -   The process of creating meaningful patterns from raw sensory information.

1.   The Nature of Sensation

     A.   The Basic Process

     B.   Sensory Thresholds

- Absolute Threshold

- Adaptation

- Difference Threshold

- Subliminal Perception

Thinking Critically: Advertising and Subconscious Messages

- Extrasensory Perception

2.   Vision

     A.   The Visual System (Draw an eye here as shown in Figure 3-2, page 100 in the textbook)

- Cornea

- Pupil

- Iris

- Lens

- Retina

- Blind Spot

- Fovea

- Receptor Cells

    - Rods

    - Cones

    - Bipolar cells

    - Visual acuity

- Adaptation

    - Dark Adaptation

    - Light Adaptation

    - Afterimage

- From Eye to Brain

    - Ganglion cells

    - Optic nerve

    - Optic chiasm

    - Feature detectors

B.   Color Vision

- Properties of color

    - Hue

    - Saturation

    - Brightness

- Theories of color vision

    - Additive color mixing

    - Subtractive color mixing

    - Trichromatic Theory

    - Color blindness

    - Opponent-Process Theory

C.   Color Vision in Other Species

3.   Hearing

A.   Sound

- Sound waves

- Frequency

- Hertz (Hz)

- Pitch

- Amplitude

- Decibel

- Overtones

- Timbre

Thinking Critically: An Ancient Question

B. The Ear

- Hammer, anvil, stirrup

- Oval window

- Round window

- Cochlea

- Basilar membrane

- Organ of Corti

- Neural Connections

C. Theories of Hearing

- Place Theory

- Frequency Theory

- Volley principle

D. Hearing Disorders

Enduring Issues: Deaf Culture

4. The Other Senses

A. Smell

- Detecting common odors

- Communicating with Pheromones

On the Cutting Edge: Do Humans Communicate with Pheromones?

B. Taste

- Vomeronasal organ (VNO)

- Taste buds

- Papillae

C. Kinesthetic and Vestibular Senses

- Stretch receptors

- Golgi tendon organs

- Vestibular senses

D. Sensations of Motion

E. The Skin Senses

F. Pain

- Individual differences

  - Gate Control Theory

  - Biopsychosocial Theory

- Alternative Approaches

  - The Placebo Effect

5. Perception

A. Perceptual Organization

B. Perceptual Constancies

Applying Psychology: How Do We See Objects and Shapes?

C. Perception of Distance and Depth

- Monocular Cues

  - Aerial perspective

  - Texture gradient

  - Linear perspective

  - Motion parallax

- Binocular Cues

  - Stereoscopic vision

  - Retinal disparity

  - Convergence

- Locating Sounds

  - Monaural cue

  - Binaural cue

D. Perception of Movement

E. Visual Illusions

F. Observer Characteristics: Individual Differences and Culture

- Motivation

- Values

- Expectations

- Cognitive Style

- Experience and Culture

- Personality

Enduring Issues: How Does Ethnicity Influence Perception?

Enduring Issues: Do Perceptual Experiences Reflect the Outside World?

Web Investigations
www.prenhall.com/morris

Chapter 3--Investigating Olfaction: The Nose Knows

Everyone has a funny (or even embarrassing) story to tell about olfaction. But consider what life would be like without a sense of smell. Some people face this challenge daily because they have lost their sense of smell. This condition is called *anosmia*. Anosmia can be the result of a genetic condition, or it may result from an injury such as a strong blow to the head. In either case, the olfactory pathway is disrupted and the sense of smell is diminished or even eliminated.

The *Web Investigations* for this chapter begin with an examination of olfactory anatomy. Once you understand the anatomy of smell, you can then examine how smell enhances taste and may change moods. You can also critically examine claims that smell can enhance sexual desire or be used in a therapeutic intervention.

To begin, go to the Morris Companion Web Site at the internet address shown above, select chapter 3, and click on **Web Investigations**. *Have fun as you learn.*

Multiple Choice Pretest

This pretest will help you identify the topics in the chapter that are most difficult for you. By focusing your study time in those areas, you will see the greatest improvement.

1. The process of sensation is _____.
   a. focused in the sympathetic nervous system
   b. the organization of stimuli into meaningful patterns
   c. the stimulation of the senses
   d. the internal activity in the absence of external stimulation

2. Creating meaningful patterns from sensory information is the process called _____.
   a. perception
   b. transduction
   c. motion parallax
   d. sensation

3. A receptor cell _____.
   a. responds to all intensities of stimulation
   b. responds to all types of energy
   c. can respond only to light energy
   d. is specialized to respond to one type of energy

4. When a stimulus can be detected 50 percent of the time it is called _____.
   a. noticeable threshold
   b. absolute threshold
   c. theoretical threshold
   d. difference threshold

5. A change in stimulation that can be detected 50 percent of the time is called _____.
   a. noticeable threshold
   b. absolute threshold
   c. theoretical threshold
   d. difference threshold

6. Messages that are supposedly sent to people which motivate them to buy a product without them being aware of the messages are called _____.
   a. subliminal messages
   b. selective perception
   c. inductive perception
   d. cognitive restructuring

7. Which of the senses ranks as the most important for humans?
   a. hearing
   b. smell
   c. vision
   d. taste

8. Light enters the eye through the _____.
   a. fovea
   b. lens
   c. pupil
   d. retina

54

9. The colored part of the eye containing a muscle which changes the size of the pupil is the
   _____.
   a. fovea   c. pupil
   b. lens   d. iris

10. The _____ adjusts its shape in order to focus on different objects at different distances
    a. fovea   c. pupil
    b. lens   d. retina

11. What kinds of receptors are found in the retina?
    a. bipolar cells and cones
    b. ganglion cells and bipolar cells
    c. rods and cones
    d. rods and ganglion cells

12. Cones are _____.
    a. receptors for black and white
    b. found mainly in the fovea
    c. more sensitive to light than rods
    d. in operation mainly at night

13. Which of the following is NOT true of the blind spot?
    a. Even a bright light can not be seen from it.
    b. It is the part of the retina with the greatest visual acuity.
    c. It is the coming together of all ganglion cells.
    d. It contains no receptors.

14. When fluid builds up in the eye and causes damage to the optic nerve and then loss of vision, the
    disorder is called _____.
    a. myopia   c. prosopagnia
    b. astigmatism   d. glaucoma

15. Some researchers believe that a lack of coordination between messages sent from M-cells and those
    sent from P-cells in the retina, may, in part, be one of the factors causing _____.
    a. dyslexia   c. night blindness
    b. glaucoma   d. aphasia

16. Mixing lights of different wavelengths to create new hues such as on a computer monitor is called
    _____.
    a. subtractive color mixing
    b. trichromatic color mixing
    c. additive color mixing
    d. blending

17. Frequency determines _____.
    a. amplitude   c. overtones
    b. pitch   d. timbre

18. The height of a sound wave represents its _____.
    a. amplitude   c. overtones
    b. pitch   d. timbre

19. Decibels are used to measure_____.
    a. amplitude   c. overtones
    b. pitch   d. loudness

20. The hammer, anvil, and stirrup are the _____.
    a. components of the cochlea
    b. bones in the middle ear
    c. muscles in the oval window
    d. receptors in the inner ear

21. The cochlea is divided lengthwise by the _____.
    a. organ of Corti
    b. vestibular apparatus
    c. basilar membrane
    d. oval window

22. What are the two major pitch discrimination theories?
    a. frequency and amplitude theories
    b. transduction and volley theories
    c. place and amplitude theories
    d. place and frequency theories

Answers and Explanations to Multiple Choice Pretest

1. c. Sensation results from the stimulation of the senses.

2. a. Perception is creating meaningful patterns from sensations

3. d. Receptors are specialized to respond to one type and sometimes also one intensity of energy.

4. b. Absolute threshold occurs when the stimulus is detected 50 percent of the time.

5. d. Difference threshold occurs when the difference between two stimuli is detected 50 percent of the time.

6. a. We are not aware of subliminal messages.

7. c. Vision is most important for humans.

8. c. Light enters the eye through the pupil.

9. d. The colored part of the eye is the iris.

10. b. Lens adjusts shape to focus at different objects at various distances.

11. c. Rods and cones are the receptors in the retina.

12. b. There are more cones in the fovea.

13. b. If an image lands on our blind spot we cannot see it.

14. d. Glaucoma results when excess fluid inside the eye causes high pressure.

15. a. Dyslexia may be lack of coordination between M-cells and P-cells.

16. c. Mixing sources of light is called additive color mixing.

17. b. Frequency of a sound wave results in our hearing a certain pitch of sound.

18. a. Height of a sound wave is the amplitude (loudness).

19. d. Loudness is measured in decibels.

20. b. Hammer, anvil, and stirrup are bones in the middle ear.

21. c. The cochlea is divided lengthwise by the basilar membrane.

22. d. Place and frequency theories explore how we hear pitch.

Learning Objectives

After you have read and studied this chapter, you should be able to complete the following statements. Exam questions will likely reflect these learning objectives.

1. Describe the difference between the absolute threshold and the difference threshold.

2. Trace the path of light from the time it enters the eye until it reaches the receptor cells.

3. Distinguish between rods and cones, and list their characteristics and functions with respect to light, color, and how they connect to other cells.

4. Describe the process of adaptation, include the phenomenon of afterimages.

5. Explain how messages entering the eye are processed in the brain.

6. Describe the three basic properties of color. Distinguish between additive and subtractive color mixing.

7. Describe the two main theories of color vision.

8. Identify the characteristics of sound.

9. Describe the structure of the ear and explain the functions of the various parts.

10. State the two theories of pitch discrimination.

11. Describe hearing disorders.

12. Summarize the theories which explain how the sense of smell is activated by chemical substances.

13. Explain the processes involved in the sense of taste and name the four primary qualities of taste.

14. Explain the importance of vestibular senses and describe the functions of the two divisions.

15. Explain how the sensations of pressure, warmth, and cold originate and how people respond to them.

16. Describe three theories of pain.

17. Discuss the principles of perceptual organization identified by the Gestaltists.

18. Define perceptual constancy and identify four kinds.

19. Describe four observer characteristics which can affect perception.

20. Identify the contributions of both monocular and binocular cues of depth.

21. Explain real movement. Define and give three examples of apparent movement.

22. Describe two kinds of visual illusions.

Short Essay Questions

Write out your answers to the following essay questions to further your mastery of the topics.

1.   Compare and contrast sensation and perception. Also describe the events that produce a sensation.

_____

_____

_____

_____

_____

_____

_____

_____

_____

_____

_____

2.   Define pitch, amplitude, decibels, overtones, and timbre.

_____

_____

_____

_____

_____

_____

_____

_____

_____

_____

3. Differentiate between hue, brightness, and saturation. Explain the difference between additive and subtractive color mixing.

_____

_____

_____

_____

_____

_____

_____

_____

_____

_____

4. Explain the causes for deafness and tinnitus.

_____

_____

_____

_____

_____

_____

_____

_____

_____

_____

_____

5. Discuss the biopsychosocial theory of pain perception. Give examples.

_____

_____

_____

_____

_____

_____

_____

_____

_____

_____

_____

Language Support

Students identified the following words from the text as needing more explanation. This page can be cut out, folded in half, and used as a bookmark for this chapter.

A

a duct	a tubular passage through which a substance can move
abundant	many
accompanying	to go with
adapt	change
adept	expert
adjacent	next to
advertising campaign	plan to promote
advocate	supporter
afterimage	picture that followed
ambiguous	uncertain
amputees	persons who have lost an arm or a leg
ancestry	persons from whom one comes from
apparently	it may be true
assessing	estimating
assume	believe
attuned	become sensitive to
audiocassette	audiotape

B

blurred	fuzzy, cloudy

C

channels	paths
chiefly	mostly
concluding	deciding
consequent	following

contends	believes, argues
contours	the outline of a body, shape or mass
contradictory	opposite
converge	to come together
conveying	communicating
coordinate	balance, harmonize with
credence	believability
cues	observation
customary	commonly practiced or used

D

deciphering	to read, interpret or make sense of
diminished	lowered
distinguish	see
dramatically	greatly
drift	float

E

ebb and flow	movement
embedded	inserted or firmly fixed
embedded	put into
emit	send out
escaped	to get out, leak
evidence	information
excruciating	very painful
exerted	to put forth a lot of effort

F

faint	weak
feats	accomplishments or achievements
fed intravenously	to feed by putting a nourishing liquid into a vein

flashed so rapidly	appeared so quickly
fooled	tricked
fraction	piece

G

geared toward	focused on
hazy appearance	to not be seen very well

H

hidden	unseen
hypothetical	imaginary

I

illumination	light
implants	something that is put in surgically
interpret	understand
intriguing	interesting

L

lent	gave
limbo	in between

M

minute	very small

O

oblige	agree
operate	act
originate	begin
overtones	qualities

P

partial	limited
particular	specific
pedestrians	persons walking on foot

perceive	to become aware of
placebos	a substance containing no medication
precisely	exactly
pretending	to make believe
profoundly	seriously
prominently	importantly
protracted	continuing for a longtime
puzzling finding	confusing discovery

Q

quivering	shaking

R

radical	major
rarely	not very often
realistic	true
reassembled	to put back together again
relevant	fitting
remarkable	impressive, amazing
remedies	medicines or therapy that relieves pain
resonate	continue to sound
roughly	about
routed	go along a path

S

selective reporting	choosing only what one wants to tell
sequentially	following in a series
shed	to give off
sinister	evil
speculated	guessed
stationary	standing still

subsequently	following in time
T	
transmitted	sent
V	
vignette	very brief story
vulnerability	weakness

Multiple Choice Posttest

After studying the text and completing the Study Guide activities, answer these questions to determine if you need to review any areas before the course exam.

1.   Sensation is to _____ as perception is to _____.
      a.   stimulation; interpretation
      b.   interpretation; stimulation
      c.   sensory ability; sensory acuity
      d.   sensory acuity; sensory ability

2.   The _____ is reached when a person can detect a stimulus 50 percent of the time.
      a.   difference threshold
      b.   just noticeable threshold
      c.   absolute threshold
      d.   separation threshold

3.   What conclusion can be drawn from independent scientific studies about the effects of hidden messages outside the laboratory?
      a.   They are potentially a powerful tool for changing consumer behavior.
      b.   Students can be advised to use subliminal messages to promote "speed learning".
      c.   They are as effective as when given in a controlled laboratory setting.
      d.   They have no significant effect on behavior.

4.   Is extrasensory perception a real phenomenon?
      a.   Yes, as demonstrated by countless controlled laboratory studies.
      b.   Perhaps, although experimentation has not yet given scientific support to its existence.
      c.   No, what appears to be ESP is merely an artifact of poorly conducted research studies.
      d.   Science cannot say now—the weight of evidence in its favor is about equal to that against it.

5.   The clear, transparent, protective coating over the front part of the eye is the _____ .
      a.   sclera   c.   iris
      b.   cornea   d.   fovea

6.   The lining inside the eye that contains the receptor cells is called the _____ .
      a.   cornea
      b.   iris
      c.   retina
      d.   fovea

7.   Receptors for light are called _____.
      a.   rods and cones
      b.   sclera and cornea
      c.   iris and cornea
      d.   iris and fovea

8.   Which of the following is true about rods?
      a.   They are responsible for night vision.
      b.   They are found mainly in the fovea.
      c.   They respond to color.
      d.   They operate mainly in the daytime.

9. The ability of the eye to distinguish fine details is called _____.
    a. visual dilation
    b. visual acuity
    c. visual sensitivity
    d. adaptation

10. A disorder called _____ results when fluid pressure builds up inside the eye and cases damage to the optic nerve.
    a. prosopagnia
    b. achromatopsia
    c. dyslexia
    d. glaucoma

11. The process of mixing various pigments together to create different colors is called _____.
    a. blending
    b. trichromatic color mixing
    c. subtractive color mixing
    d. additive color mixing

12. Research suggests that _____.
    a. both the trichromatic and opponent-process theories of color vision are valid
    b. only the opponent-process theory is valid
    c. only the trichromatic theory is valid
    d. neither the opponent-process nor the trichromatic theory is valid

13. Pitch is _____.
    a. the timbre of a sound
    b. how high or low a sound is
    c. the overtones of a sound
    d. the amplitude of a sound wave

14. Hertz is a unit of measurement of _____.
    a. the timbre of a sound
    b. how high or low a sound is
    c. the frequency of a sound
    d. the amplitude of a sound wave

15. The snail-shaped structure in the inner ear is called the _____.
    a. basilar membrane
    b. stirrup
    c. auditory lobe
    d. cochlea

16. Pitch discrimination is best accounted for by _____.
    a. the frequency theory alone
    b. the volley principle alone
    c. the frequency theory for lower frequencies and the volley principle for higher frequencies
    d. the volley principle for lower frequencies and the frequency theory for higher frequencies

17. Flavor is _____.
    a. a combination of texture and taste
    b. a combination of taste and smell
    c. taste
    d. smell

18. The _____ has the most numerous receptors.
    a. skin
    b. eye
    c. ear
    d. nose

19. Optical illusions result from distortion in _____.
    a. transduction
    b. sensation
    c. perception
    d. adaptation

20. You know a house is the same size whether you are standing right next to it or a mile away from it because of _____.
    a. the phi phenomenon
    b. the figure-ground distinction
    c. retinal disparity
    d. perceptual constancy

21. Our general method for dealing with the environment is known as _____.
    a. intelligence
    b. perceptual style
    c. personality
    d. cognitive style

22. Visual distance and depth cues that require the use of both eyes are called _____.
    a. monocular cues
    b. diocular cues
    c. binocular cues
    d. dichromatic cues

Answers and Explanations to Multiple Choice Posttest

1. a.   Sensation is the stimulation of a receptor cell, and perception is our interpretation of that stimulation.

2. c.   Absolute threshold is a sensation detected 50 percent of the time.

3. d.   Subliminal perception has not been shown to affect everyone in the same way.

4. b.   Although studies to date have not given scientific support to its existence, neither have they ruled out the idea that it might be a real phenomenon.

5. b.   The cornea is the protective coating on the outer layer of the eye.

6. c.   The retina contains the receptor cells.

7. a.   Rods and cones are receptors for light.

8. a.   Rods are specialized for dim light.

9. b.   Visual acuity refers to our ability to see fine details.

10. d.   Glaucoma is the buildup of fluid pressure in the eye and results in damage to the optic nerve.

11. c.   Mixing of pigments is called subtractive color mixing.

12. a.   Both trichromatic and opponent-process theories are valid, but at different stages of the visual process.

13. b.   Pitch is the same as tone.

14. c.   Hertz refers to the frequency of the sound wave.

15. d.   The cochlea in the inner ear is curled up like a snail.

16. c.   A combination of the two views seems best—the frequency theory at lower frequencies and volley principle at higher frequencies.

17. b.   Flavor is a combination of taste and smell.

18. a.   The skin is the largest sense organ and contains the most receptors.

19. b.   Optical illusions are the result of distortions in perception.

20. d.   Perceptual constancy enables us to see distant objects as the same size as when viewed close by.

21. d.   Our cognitive style determines how we deal with our environment.

22. c.   Binocular cues require both eyes.

4

States of Consciousness

Class and Text Notes

Consciousness - our awareness of various cognitive processes, such as sleeping, dreaming, concentrating, and making decisions.

Waking Consciousness - Mental state that encompasses the thoughts, feelings, and perceptions that occur when we are awake and reasonably alert.

Altered state of consciousness (ASC) - mental state that differs noticeably form normal waking consciousness.

1. Conscious Experience

    A. What is Waking Consciousness?

    B. Explaining Waking Consciousness

        1) The Stream of Consciousness, Revisited

        2) "The Tip-of-the-Iceberg," Reanalyzed

        3) Consciousness and Adaptation

    C. Daydreaming and Fantasy

Thinking Critically: Television, Daydreams, and Creativity

2. Sleep

On the Cutting Edge: Most of Us Need More Sleep Than We Get

    A. Circadian Cycles: The Biological Clock

        1) Disrupted Circadian Rhythms: Desynchronization

    B. The Rhythms of Sleep

    C. Sleep Disorders

        1) Sleeptalking, Sleepwalking and Night Terrors

        2) Insomnia, Apnea, and Narcolepsy

2) Marijuana

Thinking Critically: Teenage Use of Marijuana

    I.   Explaining Abuse and Addiction

        1)   Biological Factors

Enduring Issues: Is Addiction a Physical Disease?

        2)   Psychological, Social, and Cultural Factors

5.   Meditation and Hypnosis

    A.   Meditation

    B.   Hypnosis

        1)   Hypnotic Suggestions

Enduring Issues: Clinical Applications of Hypnosis

Web Investigations
www.prenhall.com/morris

Chapter 4--Drug Use, Abuse, and Addiction: Focus on Alcohol

As this chapter points out, some altered states of consciousness, like sleep and dreaming, are essential to our survival; others, such as those induced by alcohol and other psychoactive drugs, may threaten that survival. This *Web Investigation* will examine "…the most frequently used psychoactive drug in Western society…" – alcohol.

Alcohol is a drug that arguably causes more individual and social problems than other, more heavily regulated or restricted, psychoactive substances. As you work through this *Web Investigation,* you will find information about substance abuse, commonly abused substances, alcohol's effects on brain chemistry, the causes of alcohol dependency and addiction, and legislative efforts to deal with the problems of alcohol misuse.

To begin, go to the Morris Companion Web Site at the internet address shown above, select chapter 4, and click on **Web Investigations**. *Enjoy your work as you extend your learning.*

Multiple Choice Pretest

This pretest will help you identify the topics in the chapter that are most difficult for you. By focusing your study time in those areas, you will see the greatest improvement.

1. What is the relationship between awareness and consciousness?
   a. awareness is a part of consciousness
   b. consciousness is a part of awareness
   c. the two terms mean the same thing
   d. consciousness is measurable, whereas awareness is not

2. Which of the following is NOT an altered state of consciousness?
   a. meditation   c. daydreaming
   b. intoxication   d. concentration

3. Freud believed that the driving force behind all human behavior is _____.
   a. self-actualization
   b. positive reinforcement
   c. unconscious sexual/aggressive instincts
   d. human consciousness

4. Cycles of biological functions that are about 24 hours are known as _____.
   a. circadian
   b. diurnal
   c. infradian
   d. diurnal

5. Rotating shifts at work can cause _____.
   a. ulcers
   b. sleep difficulties
   c. one to eat more than usual
   d. hypervigilance

6. Protein synthesis _____ during sleep.
   a. stays the same   c. increases
   b. stops   d. decreases

7. If someone is sleeping and her eyes begin to move rapidly while still closed, we would assume that she is in the _____ stage of sleep.
   a. Stage 1
   b. Stage 2
   c. Stage 3
   d. REM

8. _____ sleep can be called paradoxical sleep.
   a. Stage 1
   b. Stage 2
   c. Stage 3
   d. REM

9. About _____ percent of the time people report vivid dreams when they are awakened in REM sleep.
   a. 20 percent   c. 60 percent
   b. 40 percent   d. 80 percent

10. Sleep terrors are most often found in _____.
    a. children under age 4
    b. children ages 4 to 12
    c. adolescents ages 12 to 18
    d. young adults ages 18 to 30

11. If you want to wake someone up, which of the following is likely to be successful?
    a. flashing a light
    b. playing an alarm
    c. saying the sleeper's name
    d. shake the bed

12. What percent of people get too little sleep?
    a. 20 percent   c. 50 percent
    b. 25 percent   d. 80 percent

13. _____ is a sleep disorder in which a person has trouble falling asleep or remaining asleep.
    a. Apnea   c. Narcolepsy
    b. Cataplexy   d. Insomnia

14. _____ is a sleep disorder in which a person falls asleep suddenly many times a day.
    a. Apnea   c. Narcolepsy
    b. Cataplexy   d. Insomnia

15. A sleep disorder characterized by breathing difficulty at night and feelings of exhaustion during the day is _____.
    a. apnea   c. narcolepsy
    b. cataplexy   d. insomnia

16. Which of the following physiological changes is most likely to occur during meditation?
    a. higher rate of metabolism
    b. increase in beta waves
    c. increase in alpha waves
    d. increase in sympathetic nervous system activity

17. Which of the following is NOT true of hypnosis?
    a. It is useful in helping smokers temporarily reduce their smoking.
    b. Recall of events under regressive hypnosis has been shown to be extremely accurate for courtroom testimony.
    c. It has been found to be more effective than morphine in alleviating certain kinds of pain.
    d. It has been shown to help hemophiliacs reduce their bleeding during dental treatment.

18. One out of every _____ deaths in the United States each year is related to smoking.
    a. 2   c. 10
    b. 6   d. 20

19. _____ is demonstrated when higher doses of a drug are required.
    a. Tolerance
    b. Potentiation
    c. Dependence
    d. Withdrawal

20. All of the following are depressants EXCEPT _____.
    a. alcohol
    b. cocaine
    c. opiates
    d. barbiturates

21. A subject in an antidepressant research study has been taking pills for 3 months. He will not find out, nor will the doctors giving him the pills, whether or not he has received the real drug or a placebo until after the study is over. The type of study he is involved in is called a _____.
    a. single-blind study
    b. double-blind study
    c. case study
    d. placebo study

Answers and Explanations to Multiple Choice Pretest

1.   a   Awareness is one state of overall consciousness.

2.   d.   Meditation, daydreaming, and intoxication are all altered states of consciousness.

3   c.   Freud believed in unconscious drives.

4.   a.   Circadian means about a day.

5.   b.   Rotating shifts at work can lead to difficulty in sleeping.

6.   c.   Protein synthesis increases during sleep.

7.   d.   REM stage of sleep means rapid eye movements.

8.   d.   REM sleep is also called paradoxical sleep because a person's brain is very active.

9.   d.   If someone is awakened during REM sleep, 80 percent of the time dreams are remembered.

10.   b.   Night terrors occur in children 4-12 years of age.

11.   c.   The best way to wake someone up is to say their name.

12.   c.   33-50% of adults do not get enough sleep.

13.   d.   Insomnia is trouble getting to sleep or staying asleep.

14.   c.   Narcolepsy is a disorder in which someone can suddenly fall asleep many times a day.

15.   a.   Someone with apnea stops breathing many times during the night.

16.   c.   Alpha brain waves result when someone is meditating.

17.   b.   Recall of information can be distorted during hypnosis which is a problem in court testimony.

18.   b.   One out of 6 deaths in America is related to smoking.

19.   a.   Requiring higher and higher amounts of a drug is called tolerance.

20.   b.   Cocaine is a stimulant not a depressant.

21.   b.   In a double-blind research study neither the subject nor the experimenter know if the subject is part of the control group or the treatment group.

Learning Objectives

After you have read and studied this chapter, you should be able to complete the following statements. Exam questions will likely reflect these learning objectives.

1. Describe how the following are related: consciousness, waking consciousness, altered states of consciousness.

2. Explain daydreaming.

3. Describe the stages of sleep and dreaming.

4. Explain why REM sleep is also called paradoxical sleep.

5. Explain the theories of the nature and content of dreams.

6. Define the sleep disorders of insomnia, narcolepsy, and apnea.

7. Explain the biological, psychology, social and cultural factors of addiction.

8. Explain the difference between substance abuse and substance dependence.

9. Describe and explain the effects of depressants, stimulants, and hallucinogens.

10. Identify two conditions that can determine the effects of drugs.

11. List two negative effects of each of the following drugs: alcohol, marijuana, amphetamines, barbiturates, the opiates, cocaine, and the hallucinogens.

12. Describe meditation and hypnosis.

Short Essay Questions

Write out your answers to the following essay questions to further your mastery of the topics.

1. Explain how circadium rhythms affect our functioning and also how disruptions in these rhythms can negatively affect people.

_____

_____

_____

_____

_____

_____

_____

_____

_____

_____

_____

_____

2. Explain the possible uses of meditation.

_____

_____

_____

_____

_____

_____

_____

_____

_____

_____

3. Describe narcolepsy, sleep apnea, and insomnia.

_____

_____

_____

_____

_____

_____

_____

_____

_____

_____

_____

4. Describe the physical and psychological effects of stimulants and the problems associated with their use.

_____

_____

_____

_____

_____

_____

_____

_____

_____

_____

_____

Language Support

Students identified the following words from the text as needing more explanation. This page can be cut out, folded in half, and used as a bookmark for this chapter.

A

accredited	certified, officially accepted
aggravate	make worse
anxious	worried
apathy	not interested in anything, bored

B

banned	not allowed

C

carnival rides	roller coaster rides, etc.
censored	changed to be more acceptable
chronic	done repeatedly for a long time
coherent	makes sense
considerable	lots of
consumption	drinking, eating, using
contaminants	poisonous parts

D

deprivation	doing without human needs
derive	get
deterrent	something that stops you
devastating	destructive, very bad
diagnosis	doctor's judgment
diminish	make less
diminished capacity	less able to
disillusioned	less satisfied, less happy about
distorted	changed

drinking binges	out of control drinking
drowsiness	sleepiness
duration	length of time, how long

E

effortless engagement	being involved and working well
elusive	hard to understand
episodes	experiences, times
episodically	from time to time, not all the time
equate	see as being the same thing
escalates	grows
essential	needed
essentially	mostly, pretty much
evolutionary standpoint	the view of the development of humans

F

fascinated	made them very interested
filter out	not pay attention to
fleeting	quickly passing
foresight	looking ahead
frequently	often
frenzied	frantic, wild
frown on	not approve

G

gastrointestinal	related to your stomach intestines

H

habitually	pretty much all the time, as a habit
harmony	getting along
hindsight	looking back

I

imagery	imaginary pictures
impaired	damaged, not working so well
impulsiveness	doing things without thinking
in conjunction with	together with
inconsequential	not very important
induced	caused
ingesting	taking
insomnia	sleeplessness, not being able to sleep
interfere	cause problems with
interspersed with	with something else between
intoxication	drunkenness, being drunk
investigators	people who find things out
irritability	getting annoyed and angry

J

joining	becoming part of

K

kaleidoscope	an overall pattern made up of very many parts

L

less profoundly	not so much
loosely connected	not making sense
lucidity	very clear

M

masked	had their eyes covered
merely	only
mimicking	copying, imitating
mirroring	the same as
motives	reasons we do things

N

negative consequences	bad results
nonproductive	not clearly useful
nonusing counterparts	those who didn't take it
not rigid	not very definite

O

overaroused	too excited, stressed

P

Paradoxically	opposite of what you would expect
plagued	very bothered
phenomenon whereby	so that, without whereby: happening
practiced	done
precede	come before
predisposed	naturally that way, more likely to
preoccupied	worried about
prescribed	medication approved by doctor
prevailing	major, primary
primitive	basic
prolonged	long lasting
prompted	started

R

reestablish	get back to
relative newcomer	pretty new
relief	better feeling
resembling	looking like
restructured	constructed again
retard	hold back
routinely	commonly, usually

rudimentary	simple

S

scenario	circumstances
shifting	changing
spontaneously	without thinking
strenuous	very active, physically demanding
striking	noticeable, strong
subsequent	later, after
suppresses	holds back, weakens
sustaining	keeping
swift	sudden, quick
switching	changing
symbolic	something instead of, one thing representing another
synthetic	not natural, man-made

U

under the watchful eye	being watched by
underlie	are the cause of

V

vulnerable to	in danger of

Multiple Choice Posttest

After studying the text and completing the Study Guide activities, answer these questions to determine if you need to review any areas before the course exam.

1. What is the relationship between awareness and consciousness?
   a. they are essentially synonymous
   b. awareness is broader in scope than consciousness
   c. consciousness is broader in scope than awareness
   d. they refer to different states of waking consiousness

2. James developed the idea of the flow of conscious ideas and information resembling a
   a. tide.
   b. lake.
   c. stream.
   d. wind.

3. How did early behaviorists view the notion of consciousness?
   a. they viewed it as necessarily central to psychology
   b. they believed that psychologists should study consciousness, but only as a peripheral interest
   c. they essentially rejected it
   d. they believed that it would become more relevant to psychologists as the discipline matured

4. Which brain structure is involved in a rapid "sweeping and scanning" process that results in a series of "moments of conciousness"?
   a. corpus callosum
   b. cerebral cortex
   c. thalamus
   d. hypothalamus

5. According to Singer, daydreams _____.
   a. are an important part of our ability to process information.
   b. are the result of unfulfilled sexual desires
   c. are the equivalent of a mental vacation from reality
   d. are a retreat from the real world and have no practical value

6. Our sleeping-waking cycle follows a _____ rhythm.
   a. ultradian
   b. monournal
   c. diurnal
   d. circadian

7. In general, within the animal kingdom, what is the relationship between body size and amount of time spent sleeping?
   a. larger animals generally sleep more
   b. there is no consistent relationship between size and amount of sleep
   c. smaller animals generally sleep more
   d. very large and very small animals sleep most, whereas mid-sized animals sleep least

8. People may be able to adjust their biological clocks to prevent jet lag by taking small amount of the hormone _____.
   a. serotonin   c. dopamine
   b. epinephrin   d. melatonin

9. Which of the following is NOT seen in REM sleep?
    a. paralysis of body muscles
    b. periods of REM sleep get shorter as the night continues
    c. rapid eye movement
    d. arousal of brain activity

10. Who sleeps the longest?
    a. infants
    b. children
    c. adolescents
    d. elderly

11. Freud believed that sleep and dreams expressed ideas that were free from _____.
    a. memories of worrisome daily events
    b. instinctive feelings of anger, jealousy, or ambition
    c. conscious controls and moral rules
    d. the impact of learning

12. Research appears to be supporting the hypothesis that REM sleep _____.
    a. reflects the brain's efforts to stimulate itself
    b. is related to restoration and growth at the neurophysiological level
    c. dreams are generated by random out bursts of nerve activity
    d. dreams reflect the brain's effort to free itself of irrelevant and repetitious thoughts

13. Which of the following is NOT a suggestion to help overcome insomnia?
    a. establish regular sleeping habits
    b. have a strong alcoholic drink before bed
    c. change bedtime routine
    d. get out of bed and do something until feeling sleepy

14. _____ is a sleep disorder in which a person has trouble falling asleep or remaining asleep.
    a. Apnea   c. Narcolepsy
    b. Cataplexy   d. Insomnia

15. _____ is a sleep disorder in which a person falls asleep suddenly many times a day.
    a. Apnea   c. Narcolepsy
    b. Cataplexy   d. Insomnia

16. A sleep disorder characterized by breathing difficulty at night and feelings of exhaustion during the day is _____.
    a. apnea   c. narcolepsy
    b. cataplexy   d. insomnia

17. In the double-blind procedure, some subjects receive a medication while the control group receives an inactive substance called _____.
    a. control treatment
    b. Hawthorne reactor
    c. a placebo
    d. dependent variable

18. Some people experience alcohol as a(n) _____ because it inhibits centers in the brain that are used in higher-level thinking and inhibition of impulsive behavior.
    a. stimulant
    b. depressant
    c. hallucinogenic
    d. antigen

19. Recent research in Denmark indicates that alcohol _____.
    a. inactivates neurotransmitters
    b. causes brain cells to dedifferentiate
    c. disconnects brain cells from each other
    d. all of the above

20. Drugs such as heroin that dull the senses and induce feelings of euphoria and relaxation are _____.
    a. hallucinogens
    b. opiates
    c. barbiturates
    d. placebos

21. All of the following are withdrawal symptoms from heavy coffee use EXCEPT _____.
    a. depression
    b. insomnia
    c. lethargy
    d. headaches

22. MDMA (Ecstasy) has been associated with:
    a. negative effects on mood, sleep, and appetite
    b. birth defects if used by expectant mothers
    c. a decrease in intelligence scores
    d. all of the above

23. Smoking increases _____ in the pleasure centers of the brain.
    a. endorphins
    b. acetylcholine
    c. dopamine
    d. norepinephrine

24. Mescaline, peyote, and psilocybin are all _____.
    a. stimulants
    c. barbiturates
    b. opiates
    d. hallucinogens

Answers and Explanations to Multiple Choice Posttest

1.   c.   Awareness is part of consiousness.

2.   c.   James described the flow of consciousness like a stream.

3.   c.   They essentially rejected the notion of consciousness.

4.   c.   The thalamus rapidly scans various brain centers producing "moments of consciousness."

5.   a.   Singer believes daydreaming is important to process information.

6.   d.   Circadian rhythms include a daily sleep and awake cycle.

7.   c.   Smaller animals generally sleep more than larger ones.

8.   d.   A small amount of melatonin may prevent jet lag.

9.   b.   Periods of REM get longer throughout the night, not shorter.

10.   a.   Infants require the most sleep.

11.   c.   Dreams were thought by Freud to be free from conscious controls and moral rules.

12.   b.   Research supports that REM sleep is involved with restoration.

13.   b.   Alcohol interferes with getting a good night's sleep.

14.   d.   Insomnia is trouble getting to sleep or staying asleep.

15.   c.   Narcolepsy is a disorder in which someone can suddenly fall asleep many times a day.

16.   a.   Someone with apnea stops breathing many times during the night.

17.   c.   A placebo is an inactive substance given to the control group.

18.   a.   Alcohol may be experienced as a stimulant because it decreases our inhibitions.

19.   c.   Alcohol may disconnect brain cells from each other.

20.   b.   Heroin is an opiate.

21.   b.   Caffeine withdrawal does not usually interfere with sleep because a person tends to be very sleepy.

22.   d.   All of the outcomes listed have been linked to MDMA use.

23.   c.   Smoking increases dopamine in the pleasure centers.

24.   d.   Mescaline, peyote and psilocybin are all hallucinogens.

5

Learning

Class and Text Notes

1. Classical Conditioning

   A. Pavlov's Conditioning Experiments

   B. Elements of Classical Conditioning

      - Unconditioned stimulus (US)

      - Unconditioned response (UR)

      - Conditioned stimulus (CS)

      - Conditioned response (CR)

   On the Cutting Edge: Classical Eyeblink Conditioning and Clues to Alzheimer's Disease

   C. Classical Conditioning In Humans

      - Desensitization therapy

   Enduring Issues: Classical Conditioning and the Immune System

   D. Classical Conditioning Is Selective

      - Conditioned food (taste) aversion

   Enduring Issues: The Evolutionary Basis of Fear

2. Operant Conditioning

   A. Elements of Operant Conditioning

      - Operant Behavior

      - Thorndike's Conditioning Experiments

      - Reinforcer

      - Punisher

      - Law of Effect

B. Types of Reinforcement

- Positive reinforcer

- Negative reinforcer

C. Punishment

Thinking Critically: Corporal Punishment

Enduring Issues: What Is Punishment?

D. Operant Conditioning Is Selective

E. Superstitious Behavior

F. Learned Helplessness

G. Shaping Behavioral Change through Biofeedback

- Biofeedback

- Neuralfeedback

3. Comparing Classical And Operant Conditioning

A. Response Acquisition

- Classical conditioning

- Operant conditioning

  - Skinner Box

  - Shaping

B. Extinction and Spontaneous Recovery

- Classical conditioning

- Operant conditioning

Applying Psychology: Modifying Your Own Behavior

C. Generalization and Discrimination

- Classical conditioning

  - Stimulus generalization

  - Stimulus discrimination

- Operant conditioning

  - Response generalization

92

4. New Learning Based on Original Learning

    A. Higher-Order Conditioning in Classical Conditioning

    B. Secondary Reinforcers in Operant Conditioning

5. Contingencies

    A. Classical Conditioning

    B. Operant Conditioning

    C. Schedules of reinforcement

        - Fixed-interval schedule

        - Variable-interval schedule

        - Fixed-ratio schedule

        - Variable-ratio schedule

Table 5-1 –Examples of Reinforcement in Everyday Life

Thinking Critically: Schedules of Reinforcement

6. Summing Up

Highlights: Shaping Behavioral Change Through Biofeedback

7. Cognitive Learning

    A. Latent Learning and Cognitive Maps

    B. Insight and Learning Sets

Enduring Issues: Human Insight

    C. Learning by Observing

        - Social learning theory

        - Observational (or vicarious) learning

        - Vicarious reinforcement and vicarious punishment

8. Cognitive Learning in Nonhumans

Web Investigations
www.prenhall.com/morris

Chapter 4--Principles of Learning in the Real World

As this chapter makes clear, learning involves an organism acting in the environment in such a way that the environment changes the behavior of the organism. The *Web Investigations* for this chapter will give you several opportunities to examine basic learning processes in a virtual laboratory setting. As you complete these investigations, think of ways that you can extend classical conditioning, operant conditioning, and modeling beyond the examples offered in your text and by the website. By working through these *Web Investigations* sequentially you will develop a more complete understanding of the processes involved in basic learning.

To begin, go to the Morris Companion Web Site at the internet site shown above, select chapter 5, and click on **Web Investigations**. Enjoy your work as you learn more about learning.

Multiple Choice Pretest

This pretest will help you identify the topics in the chapter that are most difficult for you. By focusing your study time in those areas, you will see the greatest improvement.

1. The process of learning is defined as experience resulting in _____.
    a. amplification of sensory stimuli
    b. delayed genetic behavioral contributions
    c. relatively permanent behavior change
    d. acquisition of motivation

2. Operant conditioning is another term for _____.
    a. instrumental conditioning
    b. cognitive restructuring
    c. observational learning
    d. classical conditioning

3. _____ is a technique to learn voluntary control over internal physiological processes with the aid of monitoring devices.
    a. instrumental conditioning
    b. biofeedback
    c. shaping
    d. avoidance training

4. By pairing the ringing of the bell with the presentation of meat, Pavlov trained dogs to salivate to the sound of a bell even when no meat was presented. In this experiment, the presentation of the meat was the _____.
    a. unconditioned stimulus
    b. conditioned stimulus
    c. unconditioned response
    d. conditioned response

5. You have a cat that runs to the sound of the cat food cabinet opening. The sound of the cabinet is the _____.
    a. unconditioned stimulus
    b. conditioned stimulus
    c. unconditioned response
    d. conditioned response

6. In the experiment with Little Albert, the unconditioned stimulus was _____.
    a. the experimenter
    b. the rat
    c. the loud noise
    d. the laboratory

7. Classical conditioning is relate to _____ therapy.
    a. response
    b. psychoanalytic
    c. conditioned
    d. desensitization

8. Which of the following is NOT an example of operantly learned behavior?
    a. eye blinking after a flash of light is presented
    b. a child studying in order to get a teacher's approval
    c. a rat pressing a bar after receiving food for this behavior
    d. a rat pressing a bar to avoid a shock for this behavior

9. Operant conditioning is based on the principle that behaviors occur more often when they are
    _____
    a. punished   c. reinforced
    b. modeled   d. ignored

10. Any stimulus that follows a behavior and increases the likelihood that the behavior will be repeated is called a _____.
    a. cue
    b. situational stimulus
    c. reinforcer
    d. higher-order conditioner

11. Any stimulus that follows a behavior and decreases the likelihood that the behavior will be repeated is called a _____.
    a. cue
    b. situational stimulus
    c. reinforcer
    d. punisher

12. A reinforcer that adds something rewarding is a _____.
    a. secondary reinforcer   c. triary reinforcer
    b. positive reinforcer   d. negative reinforcer

13. A reinforcer that increases the likelihood of the behavior because a person wants to avoid the reinforcer is called _____ reinforcement.
    a. secondary   c. triary
    b. positive   d. negative

14. Each of the following is true of punishment EXCEPT _____.
    a. it can make people more aggressive and hostile
    b. it teaches more desirable behavior
    c. it can disrupt the learning process
    d. the negative behavior may be only sup pressed and not changed

15. A problem that may result from avoidance training is _____.
    a. a person may continue to avoid something which no longer needs to be avoided
    b. its effects tend to last for only a short time
    c. that it may produce latent learning
    d. it tends to take effect when it is too late to make a difference in avoiding the problem situation

16. When an extinguished behavior suddenly reappears on its own, with no retraining, the process is called _____.
    a. discrimination
    b. generalization
    c. extinction
    d. spontaneous recovery

17. A person originally feared only spiders but now also fears other types of insects. These new fears are probably the result of _____.
    a. stimulus generalization
    b. response generalization
    c. obedience
    d. pain thresholds

18. Food and water are _____ .
    a. delayed reinforcers
    b. primary reinforcers
    c. secondary reinforcers
    d. direct reinforcers

19. If you work a job where you get paid a salary every 2 weeks, you are being reinforced on a _____ schedule.
    a. fixed-ratio
    b. fixed-interval
    c. variable-ratio
    d. variable-interval

20. Unannounced quizzes is an example of _____ schedules of reinforcement.
    a. fixed-ratio   c. variable
    b. fixed-interval   d. variable-interval

Answers and Explanations to Multiple Choice Pretest

1. c. Learning is defined as the relatively permanent behavioral change that results from experience.

2. a. Operant conditioning is the same thing as instrument conditioning.

3. b. Biofeedback is learning to control internal physiological responses with the aid of monitoring devices.

4. a. The meat is the unconditional stimulus.

5. b. The cat **learned** to respond to the sound of the cabinet, therefore the sound is a conditioned stimulus.

6. c. Little Albert reacted to the unconditioned (unlearned) stimulus of the loud noise.

7. d. Desensitization is classical conditioning because a person learns to associate a new response to a stimulus.

8. a. Eye blinking is an unconditioned stimulus in classical conditioning NOT operant conditioning.

9. c. Reinforcement increases the likelihood of the behavior.

10. c. Once again, reinforcement increases the likelihood of the behavior.

11. d. Punishment decreases the likelihood of the behavior.

12. b. Positive reinforcement adds a reward.

13. d. Negative reinforcement increases behavior to avoid negative consequence.

14. b. Punishment does NOT teach any new behavior.

15. a. Avoidance training is a problem if the person keeps avoiding something when he no longer needs to.

16. d. Spontaneous recovery is the return of extinguished behavior without additional training.

17. a. The new fears are the result of stimulus generalization.

18. b. Primary reinforcement is food and water.

19. b. You are on a fixed-interval schedule when you are paid a salary every 2 weeks.

20. d. Unannounced quizzes are given on a variable-interval schedule.

Learning Objectives

After you have read and studied this chapter, you should be able to complete the following statements. Exam questions will likely reflect these learning objectives.

1. Describe how classical conditioning was discovered. Define: unconditioned stimulus, unconditioned response, conditioned stimulus, and conditioned response.

2. Describe the experiment with Little Albert. Describe desensitization therapy.

3. List the factors necessary for the success of learning in classical conditioning.

4. Explain these processes: extinction, spontaneous recovery, inhibition, stimulus generalization, discrimination, and higher-order conditioning.

5. Distinguish between classical and operant conditioning.

6. Explain the principle of reinforcement. Define primary reinforcer and secondary reinforcer and give examples of each.

7. Explain the effects of delay of reinforcement.

8. Identify four schedules of reinforcement and the pattern of response associated with each.

9. Define positive reinforcement.

10. Explain how to use punishment successfully.

11. Define negative reinforcement. Explain the process of avoidance training.

12. Distinguish between cognitive learning and traditional theories of conditioning. Explain contingency theory.

13. Discuss social learning theory and its implications for human learning.

14. Define learning set and describe the phenomenon of insight learning.

Short Essay Questions

Write out your answers to the following essay questions to further your mastery of the topics.

1. Give two examples of classical conditioning in your own life, naming the US, UR, CS, and CR.

_____

_____

_____

_____

_____

_____

_____

_____

_____

_____

_____

_____

2. Describe generalization and discrimination that occur in classical conditioning.

_____

_____

_____

_____

_____

_____

_____

_____

_____

3. Explain the importance of contingencies in classical conditioning.

_____

_____

_____

_____

_____

_____

_____

_____

_____

_____

4. Explain Bandura's study on aggression.

_____

_____

_____

_____

_____

_____

_____

_____

_____

_____

5. Discuss some considerations for using punishment effectively.

_____

_____

_____

_____

_____

_____

_____

_____

_____

_____

_____

_____

Language Support

Students identified the following words from the text as needing more explanation. This page can be cut out, folded in half, and used as a bookmark for this chapter.

A

a notable exception	very different
achieve	get to
alert	wide awake, interested
alleviating	making less
attempts	tries
attributes	says that
aversion	disliking

B

be acquired	happen
boulevard	street

C

catch their breath	breathe
commands attention	is respected, makes you notice
commission	paid for how much they sell
confirm	agree with
congested	busy, lots of traffic
consequences	outcomes
consistently	almost always
constellations	groups of stars
constraints	limits, bounds
contaminated	made bad, made poisonous
corresponding	matching
cumulative	growing; building up

D

demonstrate	show
devised	set up
distinctive	noticeable, unusual
drawback	problem
drool	drip from the mouth

E

elicited	caused
emitted	done
ensuring	making sure
existing behaviors	things we already do
extensive analysis	a big scientific study and report

F

favor	do something kind for someone else
food pellets	small portions of food
forthcoming	coming
frequent	repeated

I

inadvertently	by accident, not on purpose
inappropriate	not helpful
increases the likelihood	makes it more likely to happen
indifferent	not interested in anything
inferred	known indirectly
inquiry	finding out
intact	whole; complete
irrational	not logical; foolish
insightful	suddenly understanding something
interfering	confusing, other

involuntary processes	body functions we don't think about

L

less likely to occur	probably will not happen
listless	unlively, lazy

M

maintains	keeps going
misbehavior	behaving badly, doing bad things
misdeed	bad behavior

N

nausea	a sick feeling
nibble	take very small bites

O

offensive action	bad behavior
outlives	lasts longer than

P

peck at	tap with beak
persist	keep doing
physiologist	person who studies the workings of the body
piecework basis	paid for results, not by the hour
potentially	something that may be
precisely	exactly
preliminary	earlier, done before
preparedness	readiness, being ready
preprogrammed	been born like that
previously neutral	used to not be responded to
profusely	a lot
prompted	caused
prospect	the thought of doing something in the future

R

retrieves	fetches, gets

S

salivate	produce saliva (mouth watering)
scolding	verbal punishment, yelling
seized by	grabbed by, suddenly feeling
shouting	yelling loudly
significant role	important part, big part
simplistic	very simple
slam your fist	punch with your hand
spanking	hitting
spontaneous	not expected
stamped out	will not be done any more
successive	next; one after the other
suppress	make less
sustaining	keeping

T

terminating	stopping
the extent	how much

U

underlies	is the reason for
unimportant	doesn't mean much

Multiple Choice Posttest

After studying the text and completing the Study Guide activities, answer these questions to determine if you need to review any areas before the course exam.

1. Conditioning can result in _____, which are irrational fears of particular things, activities, or situations.
    a. response generalization
    b. generalized anxieties
    c. phobias
    d. secondary reinforcement

2. In the experiment with Little Albert, the conditioned response was _____.
    a. fear of the experimenter
    b. fear of the laboratory
    c. fear of the rat
    d. fear of the loud noise

3. Why is conditioned food (or taste) aversion learning so rapid and long-lasting?
    a. it is a form of punishment
    b. such associations can increase chances of survival
    c. humans are not used to colored water
    d. accidental radiation exposure can cause serious illness

4. Any stimulus that follows a behavior and increases the likelihood that the behavior will be repeated is called a _____.
    a. cue
    b. situational stimulus
    c. reinforcer
    d. higher-order conditioner

5. Any stimulus that follows a behavior and decreases the likelihood that the behavior will be repeated is called a _____.
    a. cue
    b. situational stimulus
    c. reinforcer
    d. punisher

6. A reinforcer that adds something rewarding is a _____.
    a. secondary reinforcer
    b. positive reinforcer
    c. tertiary reinforcer
    d. negative reinforcer

7. A reinforcer that increases the likelihood of the behavior because a person wants to avoid the reinforcer is called _____ reinforcement.
    a. secondary
    b. positive
    c. triary
    d. negative

8. What is the relationship between punishment and negative reinforcement.
    a. they both can be unpleasant
    b. they have opposite effects on behavior
    c. negative reinforcement is a weaker form of punishment
    d. they are essentially the same thing

9. B.F. Skinner showed that superstitious behaviors can result from:
   a. shaping
   b. untreated high levels of anxiety
   c. chance associations between reinforcement and behaviors
   d. learned helplessness

10. _____ therapy for treating anxiety involves the pairing of relaxation training with systematic exposure to the fearful thing.
    a. Operant conditioning
    b. Shaping
    c. Aversive conditioning
    d. Desensitization

11. Taking vitamins to prevent illnesses is called _____ training.
    a. aversion
    b. avoidance
    c. shaping
    d. classical conditioning

12. Reacting to a stimulus that is similar to one that you have already learned to react to is called _____.
    a. response generalization
    b. modeling
    c. higher-order conditioning
    d. stimulus generalization

13. A dolphin learns to swim toward a blue platform but not toward another platform of a different color. This shows the concept of _____.
    a. discrimination
    b. modeling
    c. higher-order conditioning
    d. stimulus generalization

14. Which of the following is a primary reinforcer? _____.
    a. ticket to a show
    b. a buzzer
    c. money
    d. candy

15. In partial reinforcement, the plan for when to reinforce correct behaviors is called a _____.
    a. response-to-reinforcement guide
    b. token economy
    c. schedule of reinforcement
    d. reinforcement map

16. Gambling behavior is being reinforced on a _____ schedule.
    a. ratio-interval
    b. fixed-interval
    c. variable-ratio
    d. variable-interval

17. Recent studies show that rewards generally _____ intrinsic motivation and creativity.
    a. increase
    b. decrease
    c. have no effect on
    d. change the nature of

18. Learning that depends on mental processes that are not able to be observed directly is called _____ learning.
    a. cognitive
    b. neurophysiological learning
    c. secondary learning
    d. primary

19. The type of learning that involves elements suddenly coming together so that the solution to a problem is clear is called _____.
    a. latent learning
    b. insight
    c. cognitive mapping
    d. vicarious learning

20. The mental picture of an area, such as the floor plan of a building is called _____.
    a. a perceptual illusion
    b. a mental set
    c. subliminal perception
    d. a cognitive map

21. Becoming increasingly more effective in solving problems as one experiences solving problems is called _____.
    a. a learning set
    b. a response cue
    c. latent learning
    d. a response set

22. The ability to learn by observing a model or receiving instructions, without reinforcement, is called _____ theory.
    a. cognitive learning
    b. contingency
    c. social learning
    d. classical conditioning

23. An operant conditioning technique in which a learner gains control over some biological response is _____.
    a. contingency training
    b. preparedness
    c. social learning
    d. biofeedback

Answers and Explanations to Multiple Choice Posttest

1. c.   Conditioning can result in phobias.

2. c.   Conditioned (learned) to fear the rat because it was paired with a loud noise.

3. b.   Conditioned avoidance of dangerous foods affords a survival benefit.

4. c.   Reinforcement increases behavior.

5. d.   Punishment decreases the behavior.

6. b.   Positive reinforcement adds a reward.

7. d.   Negative reinforcement increases behavior to avoid a negative.

8. b.   They have opposite effect—negative reinforcement strengthens behavior while punishment weakens it.

9. c.   Superstitions come from random delivery of reinforcements.

10. d.   Desensitization involves progressive relaxation combined with systematic exposure to the feared thing.

11. b.   We take vitamins to avoid illness, therefore this is called avoidance training.

12. d.   Reacting to another stimulus is called stimulus generalization.

13. a.   Discrimination occurs when an animal is able to tell the difference between stimuli and only respond to one.

14. d.   Candy is a primary reinforcer.

15. c.   Schedule of reinforcement is when reinforcement is partial and done according to specific plans.

16. c.   Gambling is variable-ratio.

17. a.   Rewards, when applied properly, may promote creativity.

18. a.   Cognitive learning is not directly seen through behavior.

19. b.   Insight is a sudden solution to a problem.

20. d.   Mental picture is a cognitive map.

21. a.   A learning set enables us to learn by doing.

22. c.   Social learning theory explains learning from a role model.

23. d.   Biofeedback is gaining control of a biological response.

6

Memory

Class and Text Notes

- Information-processing model

1. The Sensory Registers

   A. Visual and Auditory Registers

   B. Attention

2. Short-Term Memory

   A. Capacity of STM

   B. Encoding in STM

   C. Maintaining STM

3. Long-Term Memory

   A. Capacity of LTM

   B. Encoding in LTM

   C. Serial Position Effect

   D. Maintaining LTM

      - Rote rehearsal

      - Elaborative rehearsal

      - Schemata

Thinking Critically: Elaborative Rehearsal

E. Types of LTM

   - Episodic memories

   - Semantic memories

   - Procedural memories

   - Emotional memories

   - Explicit and Implicit memory

- Priming

- Semantic memories

On the Cutting Edge – Storing Emotional Experiences

- The Tip-of-the-Tongue Phenomenon

Table 6-1 – Memory as an Information-Processing System

Thinking Critically: Types of Memory

4. The Biology of Memory

    A. How Are Memories Formed?

Enduring Issues: Effects of Stress on Body and Brain

    B. Where are Memories Stored?

5. Forgetting

    A. The Biology of Forgetting

- Decay theory

- Retrograde amnesia

    B. Experience and forgetting

- Interference

    - Retroactive interference

    - Proactive interference

- Situational Factors

- State-Dependent Memory

- The Reconstructive Process

    C. How to Reduce Forgetting

Applying Psychology: Improving Your Memory for Textbook Material

6. Special Topics in Memory

    A. Autobiographical Memory

    B. Childhood Amnesia

    C. Extraordinary Memory

D.   Flashbulb Memories

E.   Eyewitness Testimony

F.   Recovered Memories

G.   Cultural Influences on Memory

Enduring Issues: Memory and Culture

Web Investigations
www.prenhall.com/morris

Chapter 6: Test Your Memory

We have all experienced successes and failures in our ability to recall information and events. However, memory takes on critical importance when we are judging the guilt or innocence of someone accused of a crime. As Wells (1998) notes, mistaken identification of an accused becomes more problematic when the eyewitness are confident in their identification. In fact, mistaken identification may be the single most frequent reason for the wrongful conviction of an accused (Wells and Bradford, 1999). As this chapter makes clear, the process of recalling and retelling the details of an event may cause the eyewitness to create a memory for an event that didn t actually occur.

The *Web Investigation* for this chapter will give you first-hand experience with some of the problems of memory, particularly for a situation similar to one that might be involved in a crime. Be particularly attentive to the instructions in this *Investigation*, because the site will let you view the event only once (after all, how can you test your memory if you are allowed to review something over and over again?).

To begin, go to the Morris Companion Web Site at the internet address shown abovee, select chapter 6, and click on **Web Investigations**. Have an unforgettable experience as you learn more about memory.

Multiple Choice Pretest

This pretest will help you identify the topics in the chapter that are most difficult for you. By focusing your study time in those areas, you will see the greatest improvement.

1. Many psychologist find it useful to think about memory as a series of steps in which we process information, much like a compter stores and retrieves data. These steps form what is known as the _____ model.
    a.   sensory
    b.   elaborative
    c.   rote
    d.   information-processing

2. A process by which a person continues to study material even after it has been learned is called _____.
    a.   eidetic learning
    b.   mnemonic learning
    c.   semantic learning
    d.   overlearning

3. Sensory registers _____.
    a.   receive sensory information from the external world
    b.   retain past information
    c.   are measures of retention
    d.   control our attention span

4. New information replaces old information in the sensory registers through a process called _____.
    a.   forgetting
    b.   masking
    c.   hiding
    d.   selection

5. The process of selective looking, listening, smelling, and feeling is called _____.
    a.   recall
    b.   recognition
    c.   attention
    d.   social

6. Working memory and _____ mean the same thing.
    a.   eidetic memory
    b.   flashbulb memory
    c.   long-term memory
    d.   short-term memory

7. The most accurate description of short-term memory's capacity is probably to say that it can hold _____.
    a.   as much information as can be heard in 1 to 4 seconds
    b.   as much information as can be rehearsed in 1.5 to 2 seconds
    c.   between 5 and 10 bits of information
    d.   as much information as can be read in 3 to 5 seconds

8. _____ results in more material being stored in short-term memory because the information is grouped together.
   a. Categorizing
   b. Rehearsal
   c. Cueing
   d. Chunking

9. Material stored in short-term memory remains there for about _____.
   a. .25 seconds
   b. 4 microseconds
   c. 1 second
   d. 15-20 seconds

10. Repeating information over and over again to retain it in short-term memory is called _____.
    a. deep processing
    b. rote rehearsal
    c. overlearning
    d. elaborative rehearsal

11. Connecting new information to material which is already known is called _____.
    a. overlearning
    b. rote rehearsal
    c. elaborative learning
    d. chunking

12. The type of memory that is usually permanent and stores what we know is called _____.
    a. eidetic memory
    b. working memory
    c. primary memory
    d. long-term memory

13. The definition of a key term from your psychology text is most likely stored in _____ memory.
    a. elaborative
    b. episodic
    c. semantic
    d. procedural

14. The portion of long-term memory that stores specific information that has personal meaning is called _____ memory
    a. semantic
    b. eidetic
    c. rehearsal
    d. episodic

15. Research on implicit and explicit memory indicates that _____.
    a. people with amnesia are more likely to lose implicit than explicit memory
    b. anesthesia blocks out implicit, but not explicit, memories
    c. the setting in which you learned information can serve as a retrieval cue to help you later recall that material
    d. all of the above are true

16. The most important determinant of interference is _____ .
    a. similarity
    b. complexity
    c. decay
    d. rehearsal time

17. In interviewing witnesses to a bank robbery, a detective hears a different story from each witness. Witnesses recall different hair color, height, and even the number of suspects involved. The most likely explanation for these differences in the stories of the witnesses is _____ .
    a. retroactive interference
    b. proactive interference
    c. eidetic imagery
    d. reconstructive memory

18. A type of memory loss that has no known neurological cause is called _____ .
    a. proactive amnesia
    b. retrograde amnesia
    c. eidetic
    d. hysterical amnesia

Answers and Explanations to Multiple Choice Pretest

1. d. Memory is compared to a computer in the information-processing model.

2. d. Overlearning is continuing to study information after you know it.

3. a. Sensory register receives sensory information from the external world.

4. b. Masking is the replacement of old information by new information in the sensory registers.

5. c. Attention is the process of selective looking, listening, smelling, and feeling.

6. d. Working memory is the same as short-term memory.

7. b. New research indicates that short-term memory can hold what is rehearsed for 1.5 to 2.0 seconds.

8. d. Chunking is grouping information.

9. d. Information remains in short-term memory for 15-20 seconds.

10. b. Rote rehearsal is repeating something over and over again to retain it in short-term memory.

11. c. Elaborative rehearsal connects new information with familiar information already in long-term memory.

12. d. Long-term memory is relatively permanent, although it sometimes experiences decay or interference.

13. c. Semantic memory stores facts.

14. d. Episodic memory stores information with personal meaning.

15. c. The setting you learn in provides retrieval cues.

16. a. Similarity of material can lead to greater amounts of interference.

17. d. Eyewitness testimony is subject to reconstructive memory.

18. d. Hysterical amnesia is memory loss with no neurological cause.

Learning Objectives

After you have read and studied this chapter, you should be able to complete the following statements. Your exam is written based on these learning objectives.

1. Describe the path information takes from the environment to long-term memory.

2. Explain the characteristics of short-term and long-term memory.

3. Explain coding in both short-term and long-term memory.

4. Outline storage and retrieval in long-term memory.

5. Discuss explanations for forgetting.

6. Describe the different types of memory and their characteristic properties.

7. Explain the limits of memory and determine if they can be expanded.

8. Describe how information is stored and how it is organized.

9. Define "schema". How are schemata used?

10. Discuss how and why memories change over time.

11. Describe and explain the brain structures and regions that are the bases for memory.

12. Understand and use techniques for improving your memory.

13. Explain the special types of memory: semantic memories, procedural memories, emotional memories, explicit memory, implicit memory

Short Essay Questions

Write out your answers to the following eight essay questions to further your mastery of the topics.

1. Compare human memory to a computer by applying the information-processing model.

_____

_____

_____

_____

_____

_____

_____

_____

_____

_____

2. Explain how elaborative rehearsal can be useful for studying for exams.

_____

_____

_____

_____

_____

_____

_____

_____

_____

_____

3. Design two ways to demonstrate implicit memory.

_____

_____

_____

_____

_____

_____

_____

_____

_____

_____

4. List six ways you can improve your memory.

_____

_____

_____

_____

_____

_____

_____

_____

_____

_____

_____

5. Explain how information can go from sensory register to short-term and long-term memory.

_____

_____

_____

_____

_____

_____

_____

_____

_____

_____

6. Attention is important to memory. What can you do to improve your attention in class?

_____

_____

_____

_____

_____

_____

_____

_____

_____

_____

_____

7.   Differentiate among: episodic memory, semantic memory, procedural memory. Give examples.

_____

_____

_____

_____

_____

_____

_____

_____

_____

_____

_____

Language Support

Students identified the following words from the text as needing more explanation. This page can be cut out, folded in half, and used as a bookmark for this chapter.

A

acoustically	related to sound
analogous	similar to
apparent	obvious
articulate	speaks well
astonished	surprised
autopsies	examination of bodies of people who have died

B

barring	stopping
blank easel	empty piece of paper
bombards	floods, overwhelms
burglar	someone who steals

C

captured	caught
center around	are about
chessboard	difficult board game
chunk	piece
cluster	group together
composed	made up of
concussion	injury from a hit on the head
corroborative	supporting
crucial	very important, needed

D

deficiency	not enough of
desultory	pointless

digit	number
diminished	smaller
disoriented	confused
disruptions	things that get in the way
dissimilar	unlike, not alike
distinguished	told apart, differences seen or heard
doggedly	do not give up

E

effortlessly	without trying hard
eluded	got past him
enhance	make better
enormity	large size
entirely	completely
episode	event, happening
excised	removed, cut out
extract	get out
extraordinary	very good

F

fallibility	ability to be wrong
fleeting	last only a short time
fragments	parts

I

icon	picture
inadvertently	happen by mistake
incapable	unable, not able to
incident	event, happening
indistinguishable	differences cannot be made out
integrally connected	fits together well

interferes with	gets in the way
interrupted	stopped before finished

L

larcenous	evil, thieving
limited capacity	small storage

M

misplaced	lost
melodramatic	very dramatic story
mentioned	stated
modalities	types, forms

O

oblivious	does not notice
overlearning	studying more than is needed

P

particularly	specially, very
pay attention	focus
phenomena	happenings
pivotal	important, big
podium or lectern	a stand for speaker notes
predominantly	mainly
priming tasks	tasks in which people are helped some
prodigious	very good
pronounced	noticeable

R

rambling	detailed, doesn't make sense
recollection	memory, remembering
rely	depend on, be sure of
reminiscence	thinking about their life long ago

repercussions	results
roughly	almost
relevance	importance which is directly related
retrieve	get it back

S

sabotage	defeat, stop
senseless trivia	information of very little importance
similarly	in the same way
simultaneously	at the same time
skeptical	not believe easily
subsequent	coming after
surrounding	around
swerved	vehicle, such as a car, moves quickly to one side

T

trigger	remind you, help you recall

U

unreliable	not consistent, cannot be sure of

V

vast	very large
verbatim	each word exactly as heard
vividly	very clearly
volatile	makes us feel strongly

Multiple Choice Posttest

After studying the text and completing the Study Guide activities, answer these questions to determine if you need to review any areas before the course exam.

1. Researchers have shown that overlearning _____.
   a. has no appreciable positive or negative effect on memorization of material
   b. increases short-term but not long-term retention of material
   c. increases both short-term and long-term retention of material
   d. often causes people to confuse information and lowers their accurate retention of that material

2. Our visual sensation of a classmate walking past us would initially be in the _____.
   a. sensory registers
   b. short-term memory
   c. long-term memory
   d. hippocampus

3. The capacity of the sensory registers _____, whereas the duration of information in them _____.
   a. varies greatly; is very limited
   b. is virtually unlimited; varies greatly
   c. is extremely unlimited; is virtually unlimited
   d. is virtually unlimited; is very limited

4. Chunking is a means of _____.
   a. storing long-term memories
   b. immediately forgetting irrelevant details
   c. arranging details into a hierarchy from most to least important
   d. organizing information into meaningful units

5. The two primary tasks of short-term memory are:
   a. to store new information briefly and to work on that information
   b. to prevent forgetting and react emotionally to new information
   c. to filter new information and to store selected portions long term
   d. to recall important facts and to practice rhymes

6. According to the _____ theory, information gets pushed aside or confused by other information in short-term memory.
   a. interference
   b. distractor
   c. stimulus-response
   d. decay

7. Elaborative rehearsal involves _____.
   a. repeating something as well as physically acting out the concept you are trying to learn
   b. organizing basic information into meaningful units
   c. repeating something over and over again
   d. relating new information to something you already know

8. The portion of long-term memory that stores general facts and information is called _____.
   a. eidetic
   b. episodic
   c. semantic
   d. procedural

9. An item is easier to remember _____.
    a.   if it is stored in short-term memory
    b.   if it is part of our episodic memory
    c.   the more connections it has with information already in long-term memory
    d.   all of the above are true

10. While memorizing a list of words, students are exposed to the smell of garlic. If the students recall more words when there is the smell of garlic, then the effect of garlic is most likely due to _____ memory.
    a.   explicit
    b.   implicit
    c.   procedural
    d.   eidetic

11. Proactive interference of long-term memory means _____.
    a.   old material has eliminated memories of new material
    b.   old material interferes with remembering new material
    c.   new material represses short-term memories
    d.   new material interferes with remembering old material

12. When memories are not lost but are transformed into something somewhat different, it is called _____.
    a.   retroactive interference
    b.   eidetic memory
    c.   proactive interference
    d.   reconstructive memory

13. Our recollection of events that occurred in our life and when those events took place is called _____ memory.
    a.   autobiographical
    b.   reconstructive
    c.   semantic
    d.   procedural

14. Memories that concern events that are highly significant and are vividly remembered are called _____.
    a.   eyewitness images
    b.   flashbulb memories
    c.   elaborative rehearsals
    d.   eidetic images

15. Eidetic imagery is sometimes called _____.
    a.   a mnemonic device
    b.   an echo
    c.   semantic memory
    d.   photographic memory

16. We use mnemonics to _____.
    a.   block out information that is not consistent with our viewpoint
    b.   block out information that is painful
    c.   give order to information we want to learn
    d.   block out information that is useless

17. The hippocampus is important for _____.
    a. transferring information from short-term to long-term memory
    b. the retrieval of memories from long-term memory
    c. maintaining a constant level of attention
    d. the formation of short-term memory

18. Which match between form of memory and brain region is <u>not</u> correct?
    a. short term memory—prefrontal cortex
    b. procedural memory—cerebellum
    c. episodic memory—occipital cortex
    d. emotional memories—amygdala

19. A form of amnesia related to alcoholism is _____.
    a. Alzheimer's disease
    b. Milner's syndrome
    c. Korsakoff's syndrome
    d. Wernicke's syndrome

20. _____ memory tends to improve with age.
    a. Implict
    b. Eidetic
    c. Episodic
    d. Semantic

Answers and Explanations to Multiple Choice Posttest

1. c.   Overlearning increases both short-term and long-term memory.

2. a.   Visual sensations are stored in sensory memory.

3. d.   Sensory register capacity is virtually unlimited, but duration is very short.

4. d.   Chunking is organizing information into groups.

5. a.   Short term memory stores new information briefly and works on that information.

6. a.   Interference results when information gets pushed aside by other information.

7. d.   Elaborative rehearsal relates new information to something we already know.

8. c.   Semantic memory stores general information.

9. c.   An item is easier to remember if we connect it to things already in long-term memory.

10. b.   Implicit memory provides retrieval cues.

11. b.   Old material interfering with remembering new material is called proactive interference.

12. d.   Reconstructive memory changes the original memory.

13. a.   Autobiographical memory is our collection of memories for events which took place in our lives.

14. b.   We have flashbulb memories for certain important events in our lives

15. d.   Eidetic imagery is the same as photographic memory.

16. c.   Mnemonics give order to information we want to learn and thereby facilitate memory.

17. a.   Hippocampus is important to convert short-term into long-term memory.

18. c.   Episodic memories are associated with the frontal and temporal lobes, not the occipital lobe.

19. c.   Korsakoff's syndrome may include amnesia and is due to alcoholism.

20. d.   Semantic memory increases with age as we get wiser.

7

Cognition and Language

Class and Text Notes

1. The Building Blocks of Thought

    A. Language

    B. Structure of Language (Draw structure of language below-include meaning, sentences, morphemes, and phonemes; refer to Table 7-1, as needed)

    C. Images

    D. Concepts

        •   Prototypes

2. Language, Thought, and Culture

    Enduring Issues: Do We All Think Alike?

    A. Language and Cognition

    B. Is Our Language Male-dominated?

    C. Culture and Cognition

    On the Cutting Edge: Culture and Cognition

3. Nonhuman Thought and Language

    •   Animal cognition

    •   The Question of Language

    Thinking Critically: Nonhuman Cognition

4. Problem Solving

    A. The Interpretation of Problems

    B. Producing Strategies and Evaluating Progress

        •   Trial and Error

        •   Information Retrieval

        •   Algorithms

- Heuristics

C.   Obstacles to Solving Problems

Enduring Issues: Where Does Creativity Come From?

Applying Psychology: Becoming a More Skillful Problem Solver

D.   Experience and Expertise

Think Critically? Solving Problems

5.   Decision Making

A.   Logical Decision Making

B.   Decision-Making Heuristics

- Representativeness

- Availability

- Confirmation Bias

C.   Framing

D.   Decisions Under Pressure

E.   Explaining Our Decisions

- Hindsight Bias

- Counterfactual Thinking

Enduring Issues: Where Does Creativity Come From?

Web Investigations
www.prenhall.com/morris

Chapter 7: Making Sound Decisions

You should have a sense from reading this chapter that cognition is a complex task that does not always result in the correct conclusion because it can be subject to a variety of biases and fallacies. There may be many times when we need to react quickly without too much thought. During other times, however—especially for "life's big decisions"—we can take the time to carefully consider the evidence and the alternatives. The challenge is to develop effective thinking strategies. Fortunately, we can learn these strategies. The *Web Investigation* for this chapter will give you additional opportunities to examine effective thinking and to practice better decision-making skills.

To begin, go to the Morris Companion Web Site at the internet address indicated above, select chapter 7, and click on **Web Investigations**.

Multiple Choice Pretest

This pretest will help you identify the topics in the chapter that are most difficult for you. By focusing your study time in those areas, you will see the greatest improvement.

1. Thinking is a synonym for _____.
   a. sensation
   b. learning
   c. cognition
   d. organization

2. The three building blocks of thought are _____.
   a. semantics, phonemes, and morphemes
   b. cognition, feelings, and language
   c. language, images, and concepts
   d. stream of consciousness, sensory registry, and perception

3. The sounds of "th," "ch," and "ph" are _____.
   a. semantics
   b. syntax
   c. morphemes
   d. phonemes

4. Psychologists who study sign language believe that specific hand and finger positions serve in the same role as _____ do in spoken language.
   a. semantics
   b. syntax
   c. morphemes
   d. phonemes

5. The language rules that determine how sounds and words can be combined and used to communicate meaning within a language are collectively known as _____.
   a. semantics
   b. syntax
   c. morphemes
   d. grammar

6. Most concepts that people use in thinking _____.
   a. accurately account for critical differences among various images
   b. depend on the magnitude of sensory memory
   c. allow them to generalize but not to think abstractly
   d. are fuzzy and overlap with one another

7. A mental model containing the most typical features of a concept is called a(n) _____.
   a. algorithm
   b. prototype
   c. stereotype
   d. description

8. Our conception of events as we think they will probably be is called _____.
   a. a noncompensatory model
   b. a compensatory model
   c. an idealized cognitive model
   d. a prototype

9. Successive elimination of incorrect solutions to problems until the correct solution is found is called the _____ problem-solving strategy.
   a. heuristics
   b. trial and error
   c. hill-climbing
   d. information retrieval

10. The problem-solving methods that guarantee a solution are called _____.
    a. heuristics
    b. trial and error
    c. hill-climbing
    d. algorithms

11. Rules of thumb that do not guarantee a solution but may help bring one within reach are called
    _____.
    a. heuristics
    b. trial and error
    c. hill-climbing
    d. information retrieval

12. It is starting to rain and there is a very high window that is wide open. Jamie is upset because the rain is falling on her piano but she does not think to use the long handle of a broom to close the window. Jamie is exhibiting the problem of _____.
    a. inadequate means-end analysis
    b. working backward
    c. functional fixedness
    d. noncompensatory modeling

13. Huan doesn't know where he wants to go to college but he does know he does not want to live where there is snow. He should use the problem-solving technique of _____ to narrow down his choices of colleges.
    a. means-end analysis
    b. working backward
    c. locational analysis
    d. elimination

14. Research indicates that a novice can often outperform an expert _____.
    a. in situations that require the ability to use information in large, interconnected "chunks"
    b. when rigid, linear thinking is necessary to solve the problem
    c. when a novel or creative solution to a problem is required
    d. when it is crucial to recognize all the facts of a complex situation

15. A technique that encourages a group to generate a list of ideas without evaluation is called
    _____.
    a. convergent thinking
    b. brainstorming
    c. circular thinking
    d. functional thinking

16. Jennifer went to buy a car. She really wanted a red car but there was a great price on a blue car which had a lot of expensive equipment on it that she wanted. Jennifer used the _____ decision-making style when she decided to buy the blue car.
    a. compensatory model
    b. means-end analysis
    c. noncompensatory model
    d. functional analysis

Answers and Explanations to Multiple Choice Pretest

1.   c..   Thinking and cognition are largely synonymous.

2.   c.   Language, images, and concepts are important components of thought.

3.   d.   Such sounds are phonemes.

4.   c.   Morphemes are the smallest meaningful unit in a language, including sign language.

5.   d.   Grammar is the set of rules that determine how combine sounds and words to make meaning.

6.   d.   Most concepts that people use are fuzzy and overlap.

7.   b.   Prototypes consist of most typical features of a concept.

8.   c.   Idealized cognitive model refers to our thoughts about how things will probably be.

9.   b.   Trial-and-error involves successive testing of various potential solutions.

10.   d.   Algorithms ensure solutions.

11.   a.   Heuristics are "rules of thumb" that can help bring solutions nearer.

12.   c.   Functional fixedness is seeing only one use for something.

13.   d.   He can narrow down his choices by eliminating areas in which he knows he would not live.

14.   c.   Experts can sometimes be so focused on their knowledge of the situation that they miss the creative solutions.

15.   b.   Brain-storming is a process used to generate many ideas without evaluation

16.   a.   Jennifer used the compensation model of decision making because the blue car's extra equipment and good price compensated for it not being red.

Learning Objectives

After you have read and studied this chapter, you should be able to complete the following statements. Your exam is likely to be written based on learning objectives such as these.

1. Define phonemes and morphemes.

2. Define grammar and its components.

3. Distinguish between the concepts of "surface structure" and "deep structure."

4. Define cognition. Differentiate between images and concepts. Explain the use of prototypes.

5. Describe the basic steps of problem solving. List and describe the four types of solution strategies.

6. Discuss various obstacles to problem solving.

7. Describe four ways in which a person can become a better problem solver. Distinguish between divergent and convergent thinking.

8. Distinguish between problem solving and decision making.

9. Compare two models of decision making and explain why one leads to a better solution than the other.

10. Distinguish between heuristics and algorithms.

11. Describe efforts to teach primates to use language. Discuss whether it has been established that other species share our ability to acquire and use language.

12. Summarize the relationship between language and thinking. Explain Whorf's linguistic relativity hypothesis. Cite criticisms of Whorf's hypothesis.

Short Essay Questions

Write out your answers to the following four essay questions to further your mastery of the topics.

1. Explain how our concepts change as our thinking matures.

_____

_____

_____

_____

_____

_____

_____

_____

_____

_____

_____

2. What are conceptual blocks and how do they inhibit effective problem solving?

_____

_____

_____

_____

_____

_____

_____

_____

_____

_____

3. Identify and compare four different problem-solving strategies and list the advantages and disadvantages of each strategy.

_____

_____

_____

_____

_____

_____

_____

_____

_____

_____

4. Compare and contrast divergent and convergent thinking. Discuss their role in creative problem solving, as well as brainstorming.

_____

_____

_____

_____

_____

_____

_____

_____

_____

_____

Language Support

Students identified the following words from the text as needing more explanation. This page can be cut out, folded in half, and used as a bookmark for this chapter.

A

arbitrary	without much thought before
assimilated	taken into
astronauts	people who fly to other planets and the moon.
astronomer	a person who studies the stars, planets, and moons.

B

batter	the person in the game of baseball who hits the ball
blackboard	old name for board a teacher writes on; typically it is white or green

C

clarify	to make clear and understandable
clear-cut	easily understood
collide	hit
combat	fighting
compassionate	caring
composed	make up
conceding	giving
conceive	thinks up
constraints	limits
construct	make
contend	state a belief
criterion	guideline or standard

D

deliberate	on purpose
deteriorate	break down
detours	turn away from the direct route

disconfirming evidence	information that does not agree
dispute	disagreement

E

ensured	make sure it happens
equilateral	having the same length sides on all three sides
established	set up in advance
exhaust	smoke an engine puts out when it is running
experimentation	trying many different things
extensively	thoroughly
extraordinary genius	very high level of intelligence
extraterrestrial	a living organism from another planet

F

figurative language	words which only serve as an example
fostering	encouraging, helping

H

hamper	get in the way of
hinder	get in the way of
hindsight	understanding something clearly but after it has happened

I

Invent	make up

K

keenly developed	well developed
knack	special ability

L

linguistic	related to language

M

minimizing	make smaller
modify	change

noncompensatory	do not make up for

N

nonetheless	however
novice	someone who is new at something

O

obvious	easily seen
optimal	the best
overcrowding	too many in a small space

P

parentheses	"( )"
perform	do
potentially	possibly
pouring rain	heavy rain
predetermined	known before

R

rages	goes on with great energy
relevant	has meaning and importance
rich assortment	many different types
rigid	firm
rules of thumb	a set of rules to follow

S

self-reliance	relying on oneself
shortcomings	problems
shortsighted	not seeing the whole picture
shrewd	smart
step-by-step	carefully following a plan
strategy	plan
suspending	stopping

T

tactic	planned way of doing something
tangled	confused
trivial	not important

U

unambiguous	clear

W

wide range	many different

Multiple Choice Posttest

After studying the text and completing the Study Guide activities, answer these questions to determine if you need to review any areas before the course exam.

1. All of the following are ways that human language differs from nonhuman communication, *except*:
   a. human language is semantic
   b. human language is characterized by displacement
   c. human language is a means of communication
   d. human language productive—there is an almost infinitely large range of new words and phrases available to us

2. Thoughts are believed to be made of _____.
   a. semantics, phonemes, and morphemes
   b. cognition, feelings, and language
   c. language, images, and concepts
   d. stream of consciousness, sensory registry, and perception

3. The sounds of "sh," "th," and "a" are _____.
   a. semantics
   b. phonemes
   c. syntax
   d. morphemes

4. _____ consist(s) of the language rules that determine how sounds and words can be combined and used to communicate meaning within a language.
   a. Semantics
   b. Syntax
   c. Morphemes
   d. Grammar

5. The underlying meaning of a sentence is its _____.
   a. surface structure
   b. deep structure
   c. latent content
   d. semantic

6. A mental model containing the most typical features of a concept is called a(n)
   a. algorithm
   b. prototype
   c. stereotype
   d. description

7. Which best describes the current status of the idea of linguistic determinism.
   a. it has been verified by field studies
   b. although counter-intuitive, it has been shown to be valid
   c. although intuitive, its validity has been seriously questioned
   d. it has been proven false and is no longer considered by psychologists and linguists.

8. The problem-solving methods that guarantee a solution are called _____.
   a. heuristics
   b. trial and error
   c. hill-climbing
   d. algorithms

9. Your car runs out of gas and you need a funnel to pour gas into the tank. You fail to see the empty plastic milk container in your car as fulfilling your need for a funnel because of _____.
   a. inadequate means-end analysis
   b. working backward
   c. functional fixedness
   d. noncompensatory modeling

10. Jose doesn't know where he wants to buy a house but he does know he does not want to live where there is smog. He should use the problem-solving technique of _____ to narrow down his choices of cities.
    a. means-end analysis
    b. working backward
    c. locational analysis
    d. elimination

11. The technique of _____ encourages people to generate a list of ideas without evaluation those ideas.
    a. convergent thinking
    b. brainstorming
    c. circular thinking
    d. functional thinking

12. Katie went to buy a house. She really wanted a large yard but there was a good buy on a house in the best school district in the area. Katie had hoped for years that her children could go to that school so she bought the house even though it has a very small yard. She used _____ decision-making style when she decided to buy the house.
    a. compensatory model
    b. means-end analysis
    c. noncompensatory model
    d. functional analysis

13. People sometimes make decisions based on information that is most easily retrieved from memory, even though this information may not be accurate. This process of decision making is called _____.
    a. compensatory model
    b. means-end analysis
    c. the availability heuristic
    d. functional analysis

14. The tendency to look for evidence in support of a belief and to ignore evidence that would disprove a belief is called _____.
    a. the confirmation bias
    b. means-end analysis
    c. the representativeness heuristic
    d. functional analysis

15. Research has found _____.
    a. a positive correlation between superior cognitive abilities and teaching children in their native language only
    b. a positive correlation between superior cognitive abilities and bilingual education
    c. no link between language skills and cognitive abilities
    d. none of the above

Answers and Explanations to Multiple Choice Posttest

1. c.   Both human language and nonhuman communication entail communication.

2. c.   Thought is made up of language, images, and concepts.

3. b.   The basic sounds of any language are called phonemes.

4. d.   Grammar is the language rules that govern how sounds and words are combined to produce meaning.

5. b.   Deep structure refers to the underlying meaning of a sentence.

6. b.   Prototypes are mental models of concepts containing typical features.

7. c.   The linguistic determinism idea has been questioned recently and now exists in a "softened" form.

8. d.   Algorithms guarantee solutions to problems.

9. c.   Functional fixedness interferes with a person's ability to see something as useful in an unusual way.

10. d.   Elimination is a decision-making technique that narrows down the range of choices.

11. b.   Brainstorming is a means of generating many ideas without critically evaluating them

12. a.   Katie bought the house because the good school for her children *compensated* for the lack of a big yard.

13. c.   The availability heuristic entails making a decision based on the information that is most easily retrieved from memory.

14. a.   The confirmation bias involves one looking for evidence to support a belief to the exclusion of other relevant evidence.

15. b.   A positive correlations means if one item changes then the other item changes in the same direction.

8

Intelligence and Mental Abilities

Class and Text Notes

Definition of Intelligence: A general term referring to the abilities involved in learning an adaptive behavior.

1. Theories of Intelligence

    A. Early Theories: Spearman, Thurstone, and Cattell

        -   Crystallized intelligence

        -   Fluid intelligence

    B. Contemporary Theories: Sternberg, Gardner, and Goleman

        •   Sternberg - Triarchic Theory

            -   Analytical Intelligence

            -   Creative Intelligence

            -   Practical Intelligence

        •   Gardner's Theory of Multiple Intelligences

            -   Logical-mathematical intelligence

            -   Linguistic intelligence

            -   Spatial intelligence

            -   Musical intelligence

            -   Bodily-kinesthetic intelligence

            -   Interpersonal intelligence

            -   Intrapersonal intelligence

            -   Naturalist

Thinking Critically: Multiple Intelligences

        •   Goleman's Theory of Emotional Intelligence

            -   Knowing one's own emotions

148

- Managing one's emotions

- Using emotions to motivate oneself

- Recognizing the emotions of other people

- Managing relationships

    C.   Comparing the Theories

3.   Intelligence Tests

    A.   The Stanford-Binet Intelligence Scale

    B.   The Wechsler Intelligence Scales

       •   Verbal abilities

       •   Performance abilities

On the Cutting Edge: Biological Measures of Intelligence

    C.   Group Tests

Thinking Critically: School Testing

    D.   Performance Tests and Culture-Fair Tests

4.   What Makes a Good Test?

    A.   Reliability

Enduring Issues: Test Reliability and Changes in Intelligence

    B.   Validity

       •   Content validity

       •   Criterion-related validity

       •   Summing up

    C.   Criticisms of Intelligence Tests

       •   Test content and scores

       •   Use of Intelligence Tests

       •   IQ and success

Enduring Issues: Tracking the Future

5.   What Determines of Intelligence?

    A.   Heredity

B.   Environment

Applying Psychology: Intervention Programs—Do They Work?

C.   Heredity vs. Environment: Which is More Important?

Thinking Critically: The Flynn Effect

6.   Mental Abilities and Human Diversity

   A.   Gender

   B.   Culture

7.   Extremes of Intelligence

   A.   Mental Retardation

   B.   Giftedness

Enduring Issues: Not Everyone Wants to Be Special

8.   Creativity

   •   Creativity and Intelligence

   •   Creativity Tests

Web Investigations

www.prenhall.com/morris

Chapter 8: Sex Differences in the Brain

This chapter presents some interesting, challenging, and perhaps infuriating observations about differences between women and men concerning intellectual functioning. Because we place so much value on intellectual functioning, these differences can quickly become topics for emotionally charged debates. While gender differences in math and verbal abilities may be so slight as to be nonexistent, differences in spatial ability may be more meaningful. Additionally, more men than women fall at the extreme ranges of measured intellectual abilities. There is significant debate over how, when, or even *if* sex differences should be reported, especially when these differences are subject to routine misinterpretation by non-psychologists.

The *Web Investigations* for this chapter will allow you to evaluate some supposed differences in intellectual abilities by reading an article by Doreen Kimura, who speculates about the origins of sex differences in cognitive and intellectual skills.

To begin, go to the Morris Companion Web Site at the internet site noted above, select chapter 8, and click on **Web Investigations**

Multiple Choice Pretest

This pretest will help you identify the topics in the chapter that are most difficult for you. By focusing your study time in those areas, you will see the greatest improvement.

1. _____ tests measure a person's mental ability.
   a. Aptitude
   b. Social competence
   c. Apperception
   d. Intelligence

2. Tests designed to predict a person's future achievement in a specific area are called _____ tests.
   a. aptitude
   b. social competence
   c. apperception
   d. intelligence

3. The abilities involved in learning and adaptive behavior are usually labelled as _____.
   a. aptitude
   b. social competence
   c. apperception
   d. intelligence

4. The ability to focus on one's strengths, compensate for weaknesses, and seek out environments in which one can function most effectively reflect _____ intelligence, according to Sternberg.
   a. exponential
   b. componential
   c. experiential
   d. contextual

5. Gardner's approach to intelligence emphasizes _____.
   a. underlying generalized intelligence
   b. the unique abilities of each individual
   c. skills required in school
   d. physical skills

6. According to Binet's test, a child who scores as well as a typical 8-year-old has the _____ of eight.
   a. content validity
   b. basal age
   c. mental age
   d. aptitude

7. Which individual test is most often given to adults?
   a. MMPI   c. WAIS-R
   b. Stanford-Binet   d. WISC-R

8. The WAIS-R measures _____; whereas, the Stanford-Binet does not.
   a. verbal skills
   b. integration skills
   c. perceptual skills
   d. performance skills

9. The ability of a test to produce consistent and stable scores is its _____.
   a. validity
   b. standard deviation
   c. standardization
   d. reliability

10. The degree of association between two variables can be shown with a statistical measure called a _____.
    a. correlational coefficient
    b. experimental factor
    c. level of significance
    d. progressive matrices

11. A test that is valid measures _____.
    a. consistent results
    b. split-half reliability
    c. what it sets out to measure
    d. subjectivity

12. When an employment test accurately predicts how well someone will do on specific measures of important job-related skills, the test is showing good _____ validity.
    a. split-half
    b. criterion-related
    c. content
    d. performance

13. What are predictors of occupational success?
    a. IQ scores, but not school grades
    b. school grades, but not IQ scores
    c. neither IQ scores nor school grades
    d. test scores

14. The idea that heredity affects IQ is MOST supported by the high correlation between IQ scores of _____.
    a. fraternal twins reared together
    b. fraternal twins reared apart
    c. identical twins reared together
    d. identical twins reared apart

15. In the United States, the _____ Program is a large nationwide program designed to help educationally disadvantaged children.
    a. Westgate
    b. Head Start
    c. Milwaukee
    d. Stanford-Binet

16. The average IQ score is _____.
    a. 80   c. 120
    b. 100   d. 160

17. A disorder called _____ results in mental retardation and characteristic physical deformities on the hands, feet, and eyelids.
    a. PKU
    b. fragile-X syndrome
    c. hemophilia
    d. Down syndrome

Answers and Explanations to Multiple Choice Pretest

1. d. Intelligence tests actually measure ability.

2. a. Aptitude tests are designed to predict future achievement.

3. d. Abilities related to learning and adaptive behavior are referred to as intelligence.

4. d. Contextual intelligence is the ability to adjust one's strengths and weaknesses to the environment.

5. b. Gardner's theory of intelligence emphasizes seven abilities.

6. c. Scoring as a typical 8-year-old yields a mental age estimate of 8.

7. c. The WAIS-R is the most commonly used individual intelligence test.

8. d. The WAIS-R measures both verbal ability and performance.

9. d. Reliability is synonymous with consistency.

10. a. Correlation coefficients indicate degree of association.

11. c. Valid tests correctly measure what they are intended to measure.

12. b. Criterion-related validity examines how closely the test results relate to a separate measure in a specific area.

13. c. Neither IQ scores nor school grades predict occupational success.

14. d. The high correlation between identical twins raised apart supports the notion that heredity significantly impacts IQ.

15. b. The Head Start program focuses on providing a stimulating environment for preschool children ages 3-5. The program has been shown to help the child achieve better in school.

16. b. The average IQ score is 100.

17. d. Down syndrome results in mental retardation and characteristic physical deformities.

Learning Objectives

After you have read and studied this chapter, you should be able to complete the following statements. Your exam will be written based learning objectives such as these.

1. List the characteristics of intelligence as described by both laymen and psychologists.

2. Summarize the views of Spearman, Thurstone, and Cattell with respect to what constitutes intelligence.

3. Trace the development of intelligence tests from Binet through Terman, noting the contributions of each. Describe the standard procedure for the Stanford-Binet Scale.

4. Distinguish the Wechsler Adult Intelligence Scale- Revised from the Stanford-Binet. Identify the two parts of the WAIS-R.

5. Distinguish between individual and group tests. Give three examples of group tests. List the advantages and disadvantages of group tests.

6. Describe the purposes of performance tests and culture- fair tests.

7. Define reliability. Identify three techniques for measuring reliability. Explain how psychologists express reliability. How reliable are intelligence tests?

8. Define validity. What are two measure of validity?

9. Identify four criticisms of IQ tests. Distinguish between IQ scores and intelligence.

10. Explain the high correlation between IQ scores and academic performance. How well do high IQs correlate with later occupational success?

11. Summarize Tryon's experiments with rats. Explain how psychologists measure the influence of heredity on intelligence in human beings.

12. Summarize studies of prenatal nutrition and Skeels' investigation of orphanages to document the influence of environment on intelligence.

13. State Jensen's theory. List three criticisms of Jensen's research.

14. Explain the relationship between gender differences and cognitive abilities.

15. List two criteria used to identify mental retardation. List four causes of mental retardation.

16. Discuss the pros and cons of placing gifted children in special classes or schools.

Short Essay Questions

Write out your answers to the following four essay questions to further your mastery of the topics.

1. Compare the models of intelligence of Spearman, Thurstone, Sternberg and Gardner.

_____

_____

_____

_____

_____

_____

_____

_____

_____

_____

_____

_____

_____

2. Compare reliability and validity. Discuss two different types of each.

_____

_____

_____

_____

_____

_____

_____

_____

_____

_____

_____

3.   Why are some IQ tests considered unfair to certain groups of people?

_____

_____

_____

_____

_____

_____

_____

_____

_____

_____

4.   What is creativity? How is it related to intelligence?

_____

_____

_____

_____

_____

_____

_____

_____

_____

Language Support

Students identified the following words from the text as needing more explanation. This page can be cut out, folded in half, and used as a bookmark for this chapter.

A

accelerated	faster
accentuate	emphasize, point out
accurate	true
activity wheel	a wheel that animals run on for exercise
aggregate	combination
artifact of social status	false because of the effect of social status
aspects	parts
assumes	believes
astounding	very impressive

C

conflicting data	facts that do not agree
controversy	to not agree
conveys	gives
cultural norms	standards taught by our families and society

D

decade	10 years
demonstrably superior	can be shown to be better
deprivation	doing without
dimension	part
disastrous effect	terrible effect
discriminate	to tell the difference between
distinct	special and different
distinction	difference
dominates	the main focus

E

elite group	very special group of people
entirety	all of it
entity	thing
essentially	mainly
exceptional	very good
explicitly	definitely; for sure
furious controversy	high energy disagreement

G

global	wide

M

musical prodigies	children with a lot of musical talent

N

non-disabled	someone without disabilities
nonobvious	new and unique ways
notorious	famous but in a bad way
novel	new

O

obscure	not clear
origins	beginnings

P

physical deformities	something wrong with their bodies
plausible	to make sense; believable
possess	have
predicting	statement about what will happen in future
preoccupied	focused on
presumably	thought to be
profile	list used to describe

Q

quest	search

R

reflect	show
reiterated	stated again
relevant	important and meaningful
relied	depended on
rely	depend on
remarkable	surprising in a very good way
remedial	slower and more basic
reservation	not being sure
restricted environment	environment in which very little can be done

S

severely	very
simultaneously	at the same time
subsequent	following
suit	fit
surroundings	environment; where we live
systematic	doing step-by-step according to a plan

U

undernourished	not well fed
unique	unusual; different

V

virtually identical	almost identical
visual imagery	picture things in our mind
vividly	very clear and bright

W

word fluency	think of words easily

Multiple Choice Posttest

After studying the text and completing the Study Guide activities, answer these questions to determine if you need to review any areas before the course exam.

1. The concept of generalized intelligence is based on the theories of _____.
    a. Spearman
    b. Guilford
    c. Thurstone
    d. Terman

2. Tests designed to predict a person's future achievement in a specific area are called _____ tests.
    a. aptitude
    b. social competence
    c. apperception
    d. intelligence

3. Thurstone's theory of intelligence includes _____.
    a. s factors
    b. seven primary mental abilities
    c. operations, contents, and products
    d. performance

4. The ability to adjust to new tasks and situations, to gain insights, and to adapt creatively involves _____ intelligence, according to Sternberg.
    a. exponential
    b. componential
    c. experiential
    d. contextual

5. In Binet's formula for IQ, a 10-year-old child has the chronological age of _____.
    a. 8
    b. 10
    c. 12
    d. 14

6. Which of the following is NOT an individual test?
    a. SCAT   c. WAIS-R
    b. Stanford-Binet   d. WISC-R

7. The WAIS-R measures _____ and verbal ability.
    a. verbal skills
    b. integration skills
    c. perceptual skills
    d. performance skills

8. The ability of a test to get similar results when someone is retested is called _____.
    a. validity
    b. standard deviation
    c. standardization
    d. reliability

9. A statistic that shows the degree of relation- ship between two variables is called a _____.
   a. correlational coefficient
   b. experimental factor
   c. level of significance
   d. progressive matrices

10. A test that is valid measures _____.
    a. consistent results
    b. split-half reliability
    c. what it sets out to measure
    d. subjectivity

11. Culture-fair tests attempt to measure _____.
    a. cultural background
    b. the intelligence of people coming from outside the culture in which the test was devised
    c. the effects of culture on people's intellectual and creative skills
    d. the intellligence of people coming from inside the culture in which the test was devised

12. The highest correlation between IQ scores of relatives is between _____.
    a. fraternal twins reared together
    b. fraternal twins reared apart
    c. identical twins reared together
    d. identical twins reared apart

13. Which IQ score is in the mental retardation range?
    a. 50   c. 100
    b. 90   d. 160

14. A condition of significantly subaverage intelligence combined with deficiencies in adaptive behavior is called _____.
    a. attention deficit disorder
    b. schizophrenia
    c. autism
    d. mental retardation

15. Each of the following is a required procedure of the Education for All Handicapped Children Act of 1975 EXCEPT _____.
    a. a team of specialists must determine each child's educational needs
    b. handicapped children must be tested to identify their disabilities
    c. an educational program that meets the child's needs must be provided
    d. children must be mainstreamed, no matter what their disability

16. Which of the following areas is NOT in the Congressional, 1971, definition of giftedness?
    a. athletic ability
    b. fine arts
    c. leadership ability
    d. creative thinking

17. Divergent thinkers _____.
    a. quickly find the right answers
    b. score highly on the adaptive behavior scale
    c. expand on the known facts of a problem
    d. are usually highly verbal

18. Creative people are more likely than others to
    a. equally like to solve problems others have given them and problems they have uncovered themselves.
    b. only like to solve problems they have uncovered themselves.
    c. only like to solve problems others have given them.
    d. not like to solve problems at all.

Answers and Explanations to Multiple Choice Posttest

1. a.   Spearman maintained that intelligence is quite general.

2. a.   Aptitude tests are designed to predict future achievement.

3. b.   Thurstone made a list of seven primary mental abilities: spatial ability, perceptual speed, numerical ability, verbal meaning, memory, word fluency, and reasoning.

4. c.   Experiential intelligence entails the ability to adjust to new tasks and situation, gain insights, and adapt creatively.

5. b.   Chronological age is a person's actual age according to the calendar.

6. a.   SCAT is a group administered test.

7. d.   WAIS-R also measures performance skills.

8. d.   One aspect of reliability of test is consistency of scores upon retest.

9. a.   Correlation coefficient is a statistical measure of how much two variables are associated.

10. c.   Valid tests correctly measure what they are designed to measure.

11. b.   Culture-fair tests seek to measure the intelligence of people from outside the culture in which the test was devised.

12. c.   The two family members with the closest IQ scores are identical twins who are raised together because their genetic information and their environment is the most similar.

13. a.   An IQ of 50 is in the mental retardation range.

14. d.   Mental retardation entails significant subnormal intelligence with deficiencies in adaptive behavior.

15. d.   Mainstreaming is not mandated.

16. a.   Athletic ability is not a part of the definition of giftedness.

17. c.   Divergent thinkers expand on the known facts of a problem.

18. b.   Creative people tend to enjoy discovering questions themselves.

9

Motivation and Emotion

Class and Text Notes

Motive: Specific need, desire, or want, such as hunger, thirst, or achievement, that prompts goal-oriented behavior.

Emotion: Feeling, such as fear, joy, or surprise, that underlies behavior.

1. Perspectives on Motivation

    A. Instincts

    B. Drive-Reduction Theory

Thinking Critically: Primary Drives

    C. Arousal Theory

        • Yerkes-Dodson Law

Enduring Issues: The Evolutionary Basis of Arousal Seeking

    D. Intrinsic and Extrinsic Motivation

2. Hunger and Thirst

    A. Biological Factors

Enduring Issues: The Hunger Drive

    B. Cultural and Environmental Factors

    C. Eating Disorders and Obesity

        • Anorexia nervosa and bulimia nervosa

        • Obesity

Applying Psychology: The Slow (but lasting) Fix for Weight Gain

    D. Thirst

3. Sex

    A. Sexual Motivation

        • Testosterone

- Pheromones

    B.   Sexual Behavior

    C.   Sexual Orientation

4.   Other Motives

    A.   Exploration and Curiosity

    B.   Manipulation and Contact

    C.   Aggression

Thinking Critically: Culture and Aggression

- Aggression and Culture

- Gender and Aggression

    D.   Achievement

    E.   Affiliation

    F.   A Hierarchy of Motives

- Maslow (Diagram Maslow's Hierarchy of Needs; refer to Figure 9-4, as needed)

5.   Emotions

    A.   Basic Emotions

Thinking Critically: Nonverbal Communication of Emotions

Enduring Issues: Are Emotions Universal

- Happiness and Well-Being

    B.   Theories of Emotion

- Early Theories of Emotion: James-Langue and Cannon-Bard

- Cognitive Theories of Emotion

- Challenges to Cognitive Theory

6.   Nonverbal Communication of Emotion

    A.   Voice Quality

    B.   Facial Expression

    C.   Body Language

On the Cutting Edge: How the Brain Reads the Face

D. Personal Space

E. Explicit Acts

7. Gender, Culture and Emotion

A. Gender and Emotion

Enduring Issues: Holding Anger In

B. Culture and Emotion

- Display rules

Web Investigations
www.prenhall.com/morris

Exploring Academic Dishonesty

Prior to reading this chapter, if someone asked you Why do we eat? you probably would have responded, Because we are hungry, of course! Now you know that we eat because the activity of hunger centers in the hypothalamus, contributing to our subjective sense of being hungry. However, other factors enter into the motivation mix, including olfactory cues, emotional states, social influences and cultural factors. Even s imple acts like eating often have a complex web of factors that influence them. Such is the nature of motivation, or f orces that arouse the organism and direct its behavior towards a goal. Psychology has attempted to understand these forces throughout its history, especially for actions we find problematic or troubling. For example, a more complete understanding of why individuals aggress might lead to effective ways to reduce the rates of aggression in our society.

One problematic activity on college and university campuses is cheating. While cheating on exams and papers is an activity that should be discouraged, the forces that contribute to cheating offer insights into the phenomenon of motivation. It is an interesting issue to examine, because while most individuals condemn cheating and many institutions have serious sanctions against it, some students still cheat. This *Web Investigation* examines these issues and asks you to evaluate definitions of cheating and to assess various measures for dealing with academic dishonesty.

To begin, go to the Morris Companion Web Site at the internet address indicated above, select chapter 9, and click on **Web Investigations**

Multiple Choice Pretest

This pretest will help you identify the topics in the chapter that are most difficult for you. By focusing your study time in those areas, you will see the greatest improvement.

1. A(n) _____ is a need that pushes a person to work toward a specific goal.
    a. stimulus
    b. incentive
    c. behavior
    d. motive

2. A(n) _____ is an inborn, goal-directed behavior that is seen in an entire species.
    a. instinct
    b. motive
    c. drive
    d. stimulus

3. Our bodies try to maintain _____, which is a state of balance.
    a. acquiescence
    b. incentives
    c. homeostasis
    d. reciprocity

4. External stimuli that lead to goal-directed behavior are called _____.
    a. drives
    b. needs
    c. incentives
    d. reciprocals

5. All of the following are examples of primary drives EXCEPT
    a. hunger
    b. thirst
    c. money
    d. affiliation

6. Our body regulates metabolism, fat storage, and food intake to maintain a specific weight. This homeostatic mechanism is called _____.
    a. a reciprocal feedback center
    b. set point
    c. the drive reduction center
    d. the satiety center

7. Increased _____ is the most effective way to increase the body's metabolism when trying to lose weight.
    a. protein consumption
    b. reduction of calories
    c. exercise
    d. sleep

8. Lower testosterone levels can result in decreased sexual desire in _____.
    a. men only
    b. women only
    c. both men and women
    d. neither men nor women

9. Scents that can be sexually stimulating are called _____.
   a. androgens
   b. corticorsteroids
   c. globulins
   d. pheromones

10. Hiking in a cave could satisfy each of the following EXCEPT _____.
    a. exploration motive
    b. activity motive
    c. curiosity motive
    d. contact motive

11. Purposefully inflicting harm on others is known as _____ behavior.
    a. anger-driven
    b. violent
    c. aggressive
    d. confrontational

12. What typically happens when extrinsic rewards are offered for a behavior?
    a. the behavior stops
    b. intrinsic motivation for that behavior decreases
    c. the extrinsic rewards are refused
    d. the extrinsic rewards are seen as a strong incentive to continue the behavior

13. The emotion of _____ is most closely related to aggression.
    a. depression
    b. pain
    c. frustration
    d. conflict

14. Most psychologists believe that aggression is _____.
    a. an innate biological response to frustration
    b. linked to sexual drive
    c. a learned response
    d. a drive that builds up over time and must be released

15. High levels of leptin signal the brain to _____.
    a. reduce appetite
    b. decrease the rate at which fat is burned
    c. increase appetite
    d. modulate glucostatin levels

16. The _____ motive is related to the need to influence or control other people.
    a. social
    b. achievement
    c. status
    d. power

17. A need to be with other people is called a(n) _____ need.
    a. social
    b. affiliation
    c. status
    d. power

18. The highest level of motive according to Maslow is _____.
    a. physiological need
    b. self-actualization
    c. esteem needs
    d. need for success

19. The _____ theory states that emotional experience results from physiological changes caused by stimuli.
    a. James-Lange
    b. Cannon-Bard
    c. cognitive
    d. hierarchy

Answers and Explanations to Multiple Choice Pretest

1.   d.   Motives are needs that push us to behavior in goal-directed ways.

2.   a.   Instincts are inborn, goal-directed behavior that is seen in an entire species.

3.   c.   Homeostasis is a desired state of balance in the body.

4.   c.   Incentives are external stimuli that lead to goal directed behavior.

5.   c.   Primary needs are basic needs we are born with such as hunger, thirst, sexual drive, and comfort.

6.   b.   The set point is a body mechanism that tends to hold us at a specific weight.

7.   c.   Exercise is the best way to prevent metabolism from dropping when dieting.

8.   c.   Men and women both produce testosterone. Women just produce less of it.

9.   d.   Pheromones are chemically-based sexual signal scents.

10.   d.   The contact motive refers to touch.

11.   c.   Aggression is any action that hurts someone. This can be verbal and not always considered violent.

12.   b.   Extrinsic rewards typically decrease intrinsic motivation for a behavior.

13.   c.   Frustration is very closely associated with aggression.

14.   c.   Aggression is now seen as a learned response by most psychologists.

15.   a.   Leptin signals the brain to reduce appetite.

16.   d.   The power motive leads us to seek to control and influence others.

17.   b.   Social needs prompt us to desire to be around other people.

18.   b.   In Maslow's scheme self-actualization is the highest motive.

19.   a.   The James-Lange theory states that emotions results from physiological changes caused by stimuli

Learning Objectives

After you have read and studied this chapter, you should be able to complete the following statements. Your exam is likely to be written based on learning objectives similar to these.

1. Define motive and emotion and explain the roles of stimulus, behavior, and goals in motivation.

2. Identify the primary drives and their physiological bases.

3. Describe how hunger is controlled in the brain. Explain how external cues and experience influence hunger.

4. List the biological factors involved in the sex drive. Discuss psychological influences on sexual motivation. List the causes of sexual dysfunction.

5. List the characteristics of the following stimulus motives: activity, exploration, curiosity, manipulation, and contact.

6. Define aggression. Discuss three theories of aggressive behavior.

7. Explain why the need for achievement is so strong in some people.

8. Define sexual coercion and explain its effects.

9. Distinguish between the motives for power and achievement. Give an example.

10. Explain how the affiliation motives are aroused.

11. Identify the five categories in Maslow's hierarchy of motives.

12. Describe and give an example of each of the three basic categories of emotions.

13. Summarize the Yerkes-Dodson law.

14. Explain how Plutchik categorized emotions.

15. Describe and differentiate among the James-Lange, Cannon-Bard, cognitive, and Izard theories of emotion.

16. List three reasons why people may not be able or willing to report their emotions.

17. Identify several kinds of nonverbal communications. Give one example of each kind.

Short Essay Questions

Write out your answers to the following four essay questions to further your mastery of the topics.

1.   Explain drive-reduction theory and how it relates to the concept of homeostasis.

_____

_____

_____

_____

_____

_____

_____

_____

_____

_____

_____

2.   Discuss the most effective methods for losing weight and maintaining the weight loss.

_____

_____

_____

_____

_____

_____

_____

_____

_____

_____

_____

3. Summarize major theories of aggression and discuss the status of each.

_____
_____
_____
_____
_____
_____
_____
_____
_____
_____
_____
_____

4. Discuss gender differences in the experience and expression of emotion.

_____
_____
_____
_____
_____
_____
_____
_____
_____
_____
_____
_____
_____

5.　Discuss research on the topic of what makes happy people happy.

_____

_____

_____

_____

_____

_____

_____

_____

_____

_____

_____

6.　How do the actual sex lives of Americans compare to their depictions in the media?　Explain.

_____

_____

_____

_____

_____

_____

_____

_____

_____

_____

_____

Language Support

Students identified the following words from the text as needing more explanation. This page can be cut out, folded in half, and used as a bookmark for this chapter.

A

acceleration	speeding up; going faster
accomplices	working with them
affiliation	connect with other people
agile	capable of fine movement
ambiguous	not clear
ambition	strong desires
annoyed	upset
anxious	not calm
aphrodisiac	increases sexual interest
appealing	looks good
aromas	scents, smells

B

battered women	women who are hit and hurt by a family member
beeline	go straight to
betrayed	dishonored
bristled	stood up
bumpy flight	airplane that moves suddenly in several directions

C

catastrophe	major disaster
chronically	continually
cling	hold on to
coherent	organized and makes sense
contradictory	two opposites at the same time
convert	change

coupled	together with
craves	wants very much
criticized	bad things being said about a person

D

degraded	put down with words
deliberately	on purpose
dense	tightly packed together
deter	stop
diffuse	spread out
discourage	make them want to give up
distinct	different; separate
domesticated animals	animals that are comfortable living with people
drastic	extreme

E

eliciting	getting
embrace	hug
entail	involve
extracellular	outside of the cell

F

fantasies	stories in the mind
frowning	a sad facial expression

G

gory	showing horrible, bloody things
growling dog	a dog which is making a low sound to show it is angry

H

hatred	to hate
hypothetical situations	made up stories or examples

I

implicitly	by nature
impostors	people that are acting like something they are not
in the midst of	in the middle of
inaccurate	not right
infallible	never wrong
innate	born with
innuendo	hints
insignificant	not important
instantaneous	very fast
instincts	knowledge people are born with

L

larvae	early stage in insect development, like a caterpillar
less spectacular	not important
literally	truly; actually

M

manipulating	to handle with our hands
massaged	rubbed
mere	just; only
milkshake	a drink made out of milk and ice cream
mimic	look or act like

N

notion	idea

O

obtained	found
oozed	much came out from
optimum	best; ideal
oversupply	too many

P

parlor	room for entertaining friends
pickpocket	someone who steals from people's pockets and purses
plagued	bothered
portrayed	shown
predecessors	those that came before
presumed	believed
prevalent	common
puniness	very small size

R

replenish	to fill up again

S

sadism	enjoy hurting others
satiety	feeling full
says acidly	said with anger
self-preservation	to take care of oneself
sexual harassment	to feel threatened by someone's sexual words or behavior
slamming	throwing down hard
smell wafting	smell drifting out of
succumbed	lost her life to

T

terrycloth	material towels are made out of
thunderstorm	bad weather that includes light flashes and loud noises
tolerates	puts up with
triggered	started
turmoil	many problems

V

vigorous	high energy

Multiple Choice Posttest

After studying the text and completing the Study Guide activities, answer these questions to determine if you need to review any areas before the course exam.

1. We are moved toward some _____ by both motives and emotions.
    a. stimulus
    b. homeostasis
    c. action
    d. equilibrium

2. Hunger is an example of a state of tension and these are called _____.
    a. drives
    b. homeostasis
    c. impulse
    d. instinct

3. Married persons are typically _____ their sex lives than are unmarried persons.
    a. less satisfied with
    b. more satisfied with
    c. more open regarding
    d. less open regarding

4. A difference in animal and human sex drives is that _____.
    a. human sex drive is controlled by the male's reproductive system
    b. humans are able to be interested in sex at any time
    c. human sex drive is controlled by hormones
    d. human sex drive is controlled by the females' reproductive system

5. Men tend to be more sexually aroused by _____.
    a. visual cues
    b. auditory cues
    c. olfactory cues
    d. touch

6. Women tend to be more sexually aroused by _____.
    a. visual cues
    b. auditory cues
    c. olfactory cues
    d. touch

7. The biological theory of sexual orientation is unable to account for _____.
    a. the profound influence of socialization on sexual orientation
    b. significant cross-cultural variation in rates of homosexuality
    c. success of therapeutic interventions to change sexual orientation
    d. all of the above

8. _____ is (are) key to understanding the apparent contradiction between the apparent universality of emotions and people's confusion about the emotions being expressed by people in other cultures.
    a. Sensorimotor feedback
    b. Affiliation motives
    c. Display rules
    d. Satuation

9. A need to be with other people is called a(n) _____ need.
   a. social
   b. affiliation
   c. status
   d. power

10. The most basic level of motive according to Maslow is _____.
    a. physiological need
    b. self-actualization
    c. esteem needs
    d. need for success

11 In Harlow's classic experiments, when the infant monkeys were frightened they ran to a surrogate "mother" that offered _____.
   a. food and warmth
   b. food only
   c. warmth only
   d. warmth and closeness

12. According to research done by the FBI, about _____ percent of families experience some form of violence.
    a. 25
    b. 45
    c. 65
    d. 85

13. Bandura describes the relationship between frustration and aggression as which of the following?
    a. Unintentional interference with a task will lead people to become more aggressive.
    b. Frustration generates aggression only in those people who have learned aggression as a coping mechanism.
    c. Frustration almost always leads to aggression.
    d. Frustration is the least important among several types of experiences that can provoke aggression.

14. Women who have been forced to have sex frequently experience the symptoms of _____.
    a. generalized anxiety disorder
    b. bipolar disorder
    c. post-traumatic stress disorder
    d. obsessive-compulsive disorder

15. Which of the following is likely to be significantly affected by emotional level according to the Yerkes-Dodson law?
    a. watching T.V.
    b. gardening
    c. taking the college board exams
    d. taking notes in an introductory psychology class

16. The theory which maintains that emotions are caused by the interaction of physiological processes and perception of the situation is the _____ theory.
    a. James-Lange
    b. activation theory
    c. Cannon-Bard theory
    d. cognitive theory

Answers and Explanations to Multiple Choice Posttest

1. c.   Both motives and emotions motivate us to take action.

2. a.   Tensions such as hunger are called drives.

3. b.   Married person are generally more satisfied with their sex lives than are unmarried persons.

4. b.   Unlike most non-human species, humans are able to be interested in sex at any time.

5. a.   Men are more sexually aroused by visual cues.

6. d.   Women are more sexually aroused by touch.

7. d.   Biological theories of sexual orientation cannot account for each of the first three listed.

8. b.   Display rules help us to understand cultural differences in the expression of emotion.

9. b.   Social motives prompt us to want to be with other people.

10. a.   In Maslow's scheme, physiological needs are at the bottom of the hierarchy.

11. d.   Infant monkeys sought warmth and closeness from the cloth mother.

12. a.   About 25% of families experience some sort of violence.

13. b.   Aggression is likely to result from frustration when no more effective coping strategy has been learned.

14. c.   Post-traumatic stress disorder can result in women who are repeatedly coerced to participate in sexual behavior.

15. c.   Yerkes-Dodson Law states that the more complex the task, the lower the level of arousal that can be tolerated before performance deteriorates.

16. d.   The cognitive theory of emotions maintains that emotions result from a combination of physiological factors and how a situation is perceived.

10

Life Span Development

Class and Text Notes

1. Methods in Developmental Psychology

    A. Cross-sectional study

    B. Longitudinal Study

    C. Biographical or retrospective study

2. Prenatal Development

    A. Embryo

    B. Fetus

    C. Placenta

    D. Critical Period

    E. Terotogens

    F. Fetal Alcohol Syndrome (FAS)

3. The Newborn Baby

    A. Reflexes

    B. Temperament

Enduring Issues: Different from Birth

    C. Perceptual Abilities

        • Vision

        • Depth perception

        • Other senses

4. Infancy and Childhood

    A. Physical Development

    B. Motor Development

C. Cognitive Development

- Sensory-Motor Stage (birth to 2 years)

    - Object permanence

- Preoperational Stage (2-7 years)

    - Egocentric

- Concrete Operations (7-11 years)

    - Conservation

- Formal Operations (11-15 years)

- Criticisms of Piaget's Theory

D. Moral Development

- Preconventional

- Conventional

- Postconventional

E. Language Development

- Babbling

- Holophrases

- Theories of language development

    - Reward

    - Language acquisition device

- Bilingualism and the Development of a Second Language

On the Cutting Edge: The Evolution of Language from a Neuroscience Perspective

F. Social Development

- Parent-Child Relationships in Infancy: Development of Attachment

    - Attachment

    - Autonomy

    - Socialization

- Parent-Child Relationships in Childhood

    - Authoritarian

- Permissive-indifferent

- Permissive-indulgent

- Authoritative

- Relationships with other children

 - Solitary play

 - Parallel play

 - Cooperative play

 - Peer group

- Children in Dual-Career Families

G. Sex-Role Development

 - Gender identity

 - Gender constancy

 - Gender-role awareness

 - Gender stereotypes

 - Sex-typed behavior

Enduring Issues: Sex-Typed Behavior

H.   Television and Children

Thinking Critically: Television's Effects

5. Adolescence

A. Physical Changes

- Growth spurt

 1. Sexual development

  - Puberty

  - Menarche

 2. Early and late developers

 3. Adolescent sexual activity

 4. Teenage pregnancy and childrearing

B. Cognitive Changes

186

- Imaginary audience

- Personal fable

C. Personality and Social Development

- How "stormy and stressful" is adolescence?

D. Forming and Identity

- Relationships with peers

- Relationships with parents

E. Some Problems of Adolescence

- Declines in self-esteem

- Depression and suicide

- Youth violence

6. Adulthood

A. Love, Partnerships, and Parenting

- Forming partnerships

B. Parenthood

Applying Psychology: Resolving Conflicts in Intimate Relationships

C. Ending a relationship

D. The World of Work

E. Cognitive Changes

F. Personality Changes

Enduring Issues: The "Change of Life"

7. Late Adulthood

A. Physical Changes

B. Social Development

- Retirement; Sexual Behavior

C. Cognitive Changes

- Alzheimer's Disease

D. Facing the End of Life

Web Investigations
www.prenhall.com/morris

Chapter 10: Tick-Tock Goes the Social and Biological Clock

You are not the same person today that you were five or ten years ago. You probably won t be the same person five, ten, or twenty years from now. People change with age, and as they do so, they collect important life experiences that make them the people that they are. In this chapter, you have read about the many physical, cognitive, and social changes that you have already experienced. Organized by the following four events: Birth and Life Expectancy, Puberty, Marriage, and Children, this *Web Investigation* will permit you to consider how important biological events, such as birth, puberty, and birth of a first child, are related to the culturally-prescribed timing for important social events, such as college attendance, marriage, and maternity/paternity leave from work. You will encounter issues related to your longevity, and the social and biological clocks that both describe and influence so much of human development.

To begin, go to the Morris Companion Web Site at the internet address shown above, select chapter 10, and click on **Web Investigations**.

Multiple Choice Pretest

This pretest will help you identify the topics in the chapter that are most difficult for you. By focusing your study time in those areas, you will see the greatest improvement.

1. A health psychologist is interested in determining if an inability to cope with stress during adolescence is correlated with an inability to cope with stress in adulthood. She assesses coping skills in a group of 100 adolescents and then contacts the same people 10 years later. This is a(n) _____ study.
   a. experimental
   b. cross-sectional
   c. longitudinal
   d. biographical

2. When a sample of people of various ages are part of a research study done at one point in time, this study is utilizing the _____ method.
   a. experimental
   b. cross-sectional
   c. longitudinal
   d. biographical

3. A group of people born during the same period of time is called _____.
   a. a cohort
   b. a peerage
   c. a cross-sectional group
   d. a convergent group

4. The _____ period of development is from conception to birth.
   a. natal
   b. zygote
   c. embryo
   d. prenatal

5. The structure that attaches a fetus to its mother's uterus and provides nourishment is called the _____.
   a. amniotic sac
   b. fallopian tube
   c. placenta
   d. structuralism

6. A child has facial deformities, heart defects, cognitive impairments, and stunted growth. The child likely suffers from _____.
   a. prematurity
   b. fetal alcohol syndrome
   c. contact deficiencies
   d. none of the above

7. Rachel is a strong-willed child who is moody and intense. She often throws temper tantrums, and adapts poorly to change. Her temperament can be described as _____.
   a. difficult
   b. predictable
   c. easy
   d. slow-to-warm-up

189

8. Jean Piaget is most famous for his theory of _____ development.
    a. moral
    b. motor
    c. language
    d. cognitive

9. Which of the following is the correct order for Piaget's four stages of development?
    a. preoperational, sensory-motor, concrete operations, formal operation
    b. concrete operations, preoperational, sensory-motor, formal operation
    c. sensory-motor, preoperational, concrete operations, formal operation
    d. preoperational, concrete operations, sensory-motor, formal operation

10. An individual who perceives everything from their own perceptive is exhibiting _____.
    a. conservation
    b. ethnocentrism
    c. egocentrism
    d. anthropomorphism

11. Lawrence Kohlberg developed a theory of _____.
    a. cognitive development
    b. correlational coefficients
    c. longitudinal research
    d. moral development

12. Conflicts over what is moral and what is legal are likely to occur during the _____ level of moral thinking.
    a. concrete operational
    b. preconventional
    c. conventional
    d. postconventional

13. Researchers who study language development in deaf children who have deaf parents have found that the children _____.
    a. babble with their hands
    b. do not babble at all
    c. babble like other infants for a short while, but quickly stop
    d. babble verbally

14. The process of _____ teaches children what behaviors and attitudes are appropriate in their family, friends, and culture.
    a. attachment
    b. imprinting
    c. socialization
    d. autonomy

15. Authoritarian parents are to _____ children as permissive parents are to _____ children.
    a. distrustful; assertive
    b. passive; assertive
    c. inquisitive; withdrawn
    d. distrustful; dependent

16. Other than sleeping, children spend the most time _____.
    a. in school
    b. watching TV
    c. playing with toys
    d. playing with friends

Answers and Explanations to Multiple Choice Pretest

1.   c.   Longitudinal research studies the same people over a long period of time.

2.   b.   Cross-sectional research studies people of different ages at one point in time.

3.   a.   Cohort members are all about the same age.

4   d.   Prenatal development spans the period from conception to birth.

5.   c.   The placenta attaches the unborn child to its mother's uterus.

6.   b.   Fetal alcohol syndrome results when the mother of the fetus consumes too much alcohol.

7.   a.   The description is of a child with a difficult temperament.

8.   d.   Piaget developed an important theory of cognitive development.

9.   c.   Sensory motor development is the first stage in Piaget's theory.

10.   c.   Egocentrism is seeing everything from one's own perspective.

11.   d.   Kohlberg developed a theory of moral development.

12.   d.   Postconventional moral reasoning focuses on principles such as justice, liberty, and equality.

13.   a.   Deaf children of deaf parents babble with their hands.

14.   c.   Socialization is the process of learning appropriate behaviors and attitudes.

15.   d.   Children of authoritarian parents tend to be distrustful; those with permissive parents become dependent.

16.   b.   Children only watch television more than they do anything else, besides sleeping.

Learning Objectives

After you have read and studied this chapter, you should be able to complete the following statements. Your exam is written based on these learning objectives.

1. Describe the prenatal environment.

2. Describe the physical and motor development of the newborn baby.

3. Describe the perceptual development of a baby. How does object perception change?

4. What are some of the factors influencing depth perception in infants?

5. What are the four stages of Piaget's theory of cognitive development?

6. List four factors associated with the social development of a child.

7. Trace language development from infancy through age 5 or 6.

8. Explain the critical periods in language development.

9. Explain the importance of secure attachments between a caregiver and child.

10. Describe how children learn such values as friendship.

11. Explain how sex-role identity is formed.

12. Summarize the important physical changes that the adolescent undergoes during puberty.

13. Describe the cognitive development of adolescents.

14. Describe the sequence of social development from the start of adolescence though young adulthood.

15. Discuss four problems of adolescence: self-esteem, depression, suicide, and eating disorders.

16. Distinguish between the longitudinal and cross-sectional methods as they relate to the study of adulthood. List the disadvantages of the methods and how the disadvantages can be overcome.

17. Identify the central concerns and crises that characterize the young, middle, and late adulthood stages.

18. Summarize the physiological changes that people undergo as they age.

19. Identify the changes in cognitive development that people undergo as they age.

20. Summarize the differences in the ways men and women in young, middle, and later adulthood approach friendship, marriage, sexuality, parenthood, divorce, death of a spouse, and work.

21. List the factors that influence attitudes toward retirement.

22. Identify Elisabeth Kubler-Ross' five sequential stages though which people pass as they react to their own impending death.

Short Essay Questions

Write out your answers to the following eight essay questions to further your mastery of the topics.

1.   Compare the longitudinal, cross-sectional, and biographical approaches to studying development.

_____

_____

_____

_____

_____

_____

_____

_____

_____

_____

2.   Define maturation and discuss the factors that affect it.

_____

_____

_____

_____

_____

_____

_____

_____

_____

_____

3. Explain Kohlberg's theory of moral development. What are some criticisms of Kohlberg's theory?

_____

_____

_____

_____

_____

_____

_____

_____

_____

_____

_____

4. Compare and contrast the major theories of language development in children.

_____

_____

_____

_____

_____

_____

_____

_____

_____

_____

_____

_____

5. Discuss Piaget's four stages of cognitive development.

_____

_____

_____

_____

_____

_____

_____

_____

_____

_____

_____

6. Discuss the impact of bilingualism on the language and learning abilities of children.

_____

_____

_____

_____

_____

_____

_____

_____

_____

_____

_____

7. Describe the effects of divorce on adults.

_____

_____

_____

_____

_____

_____

_____

_____

_____

_____

8. Discuss some strategies for resolving conflicts in intimate relationships.

_____

_____

_____

_____

_____

_____

_____

_____

_____

_____

Language Support

Students identified the following words from the text as needing more explanation. This page can be cut out, folded in half, and used as a bookmark for this chapter.

A

abrupt	sudden
accustomed	used to
acquisition	to gain or acquire
alleviating	get rid of; stop
approaches	different ways of doing things
aspirations	future goals and dreams
assumption	to believe
attains	reaches; acquires
attributed	state the cause of
autonomy	to work alone

C

chaos	confusion
checkerboard	a pattern in cloth of light and dark small squares
cling	hang on to
collaborators	people who work together
colleagues	co-workers
congenital	happen during fetal development
contradicts	goes against
coos	make happy baby sounds
criminal behavior	actions which break the law

D

dashing	hurting
depersonalization	not treated with the respect a person should receive
devastating	very bad

dictates	demands
dimension	aspect; part
disastrous	very bad
discerned	developed
disproportionate	not equal number
distinguish	see differences between

E

entitlement	things we are supposed to have
evidence	proof

F

fascinated	very interested in

G

gangly look	long, thin legs and arms

H

heighten conflicts	increase disagreements
hollow ball	ball which is empty in the middle

I

illustrate	show
inadequate	not enough
incubator	a place where a newborn can be kept warm
indignity	not treated with respect
influential	to have impact
inhibited	not willing to do many things
innate	to be born with
intonation	use various voice tones
investigate	study
invulnerable	to feel nothing can hurt them

J

joints stiffen — bones are not able to move as well

L

loud wails — to cry loudly

M

magnified — to get bigger

milestones — important points

mittens — similar to gloves for the hands

modified — changed

moody — sometimes get sad and grumpy

mortality — death

N

nondescript — does not describe

notoriously — well known to be

nourished — feed

O

oblivious — not noticing

orient — get used to

P

perpetuate — keep it going

posed — stated

possessive words — words which show who something belongs to

postpone — to do later

pressing concern — important issue

profound — very important

prosocial behavior — actions that help other people

R

rattle — baby's toy which makes a noise

reared	to grown up in
rent	torn
replied	answered
reproduce	to make again
reserved	quiet
revere	respect
rigidly	firmly; not flexible
rudimentary	basic
runway	pathway

S

sacrificing	giving up
shallow	not deep
siblings	brothers or sisters
skipping	walking and hopping
subtle deception	to fool someone without being obvious

T

taboo	prohibited; banned
timid	shy
turmoil	upset

U

undifferentiated	not developed
unpopularity	not being liked by other people

V

vanishes	goes away
victimized	to be hurt by others
virtually everything	almost all

Multiple Choice Posttest

After studying the text and completing the Study Guide activities, answer these questions to determine if you need to review any areas before the course exam.

1. People born during the same period of historical time constitute _____.
   a. a cohort
   b. a peerage
   c. a cross-sectional group
   d. a convergent group

2. Concrete operational stage is to _____ as formal operational stages is to _____.
   a. abstract; logical
   b. logical; abstract
   c. conservation; centration
   d. egocentrism; ethnocentrism

3. _____ refers to an individual who perceives everything from his or her own perspective.
   a. Conservation
   b. Ethnocentrism
   c. Egocentrism
   d. Anthropomorphism

4. Focusing on the resulting concrete consequences of a behavior is demonstrated in the _____ level of moral thinking.
   a. concrete operational
   b. preconventional
   c. conventional
   d. postconventional

5. The _____ process teaches children what behaviors and attitudes are appropriate in their family, friends, and culture.
   a. attachment
   b. imprinting
   c. socialization
   d. autonomy

6. Authoritative parents are to _____ children as permissive parents are to _____ children.
   a. distrustful; assertive
   b. passive; assertive
   c. self-reliant; dependent
   d. distrustful; dependent

7. The onset of sexual maturation in adolescence is known as _____.
   a. the growth spurt
   b. maturation
   c. atrophy
   d. puberty

8. Menarche is the _____.
   a. beginning of adolescence
   b. production of sperm cells
   c. onset of menstruation
   d. appearance of pubic hair

9. Due to _____ many adolescents believe that they are invulnerable to danger.
   a. role diffusion
   b. the adolescent delusion
   c. the personal fable
   d. animism

10. What percent of adolescents drop out of high school?
    a. 5-10
    b. 10-15
    c. 15-30
    d. 30-40

11. According to Erikson, developing a stable sense of self and making the transition from dependence on others to dependence on oneself is called _____.
    a. self-actualization
    b. identity formation
    c. the personal fable
    d. identity diffusion

12. Rebecca is attending community college to explore various career choices and has put off making a career decision. She BEST fits the description of a(n) _____.
    a. identity achiever
    b. identity diffusion
    c. identity foreclosure
    d. identity moratorium

13. The suicide rate among adolescents has increased by _____ percent since 1950.
    a. 30
    b. 50
    c. 100
    d. 300

14. _____ is an eating disorder that involves eating excessive amounts of food followed by purging to get rid of the food.
    a. Hypoglycemia
    b. Anorexia nervosa
    c. Bulimia
    d. Depression

15. According to Erikson, young people are not capable of truly loving someone until they have developed _____.
    a. a sense of identity
    b. compassion
    c. sexual maturity
    d. formal operational thought

16. Most older couples report that the BEST years of their marriage were the years _____.
    a. when they were newlyweds
    b. when their children were young
    c. when their children were teenagers
    d. after their children had grown and left home

17. The majority of older adults are _____.
    a.   impotent and incapable of sexual response
    b.   uninterested in sex
    c.   sexually active
    d.   none of the above

18. Kubler-Ross describes the sequence of stages of dying as _____.
    a.   anger, denial, depression, bargaining, acceptance
    b.   denial, anger, bargaining, depression, acceptance
    c.   denial, bargaining, depression, anger, acceptance
    d.   anger, bargaining, depression, denial, acceptance

19. Which of the following is NOT a predictor of violent behavior in a young person?
    a.   receiving harsh punishment in childhood
    b.   a family history of violence
    c.   having a history of impulsive and fearless behavior
    d.   having Down syndrome

Answers and Explanations to Multiple Choice Posttest

1.   a.   Members of a given cohort are, by definition, about the same age.

2.   b.   Concrete operational thinking is logical whereas formal operational thought is abstract.

3.   c.   Egocentric thought perceiving everything from one's own perspective.

4.   b.   A person at the preconventional moral developmental stage focuses on the concrete consequence of their behavior, and not the larger moral issues.

5.   c.   Socialization is learning appropriate attitudes and behavior for one's family and culture.

6.   c.   Authoritative parents foster distrust in their children; permissive parents can produce dependence in their children.

7.   d.   Puberty is the onset of sexual maturation in adolescence.

8.   c.   Menarche is the onset of menstruation.

9.   c.   A belief that one is invulnerable to danger can be an outgrowth of what has been called the personal fable.

10.   c.   Between 15 and 30 percent of adolescents drop out of high school.

11.   b.   Developing a stable sense of self is key to identify formation.

12.   d.   Going to college or into the military service to explore career possibilities gives people time off before making any final identity decisions.

13.   d.   The suicide rate for adolescents has increased by 300 percent since 1950.

14.   c.   The binge-purge cycle is associated with bulimia.

15.   a.   A sense of identity is a prerequisite for mature, unselfish love, according to Erikson.

16.   d.   Most older couples report the best years of their marriage to be those after their children had grown and left home.

17.   c.   The majority of older adults are sexually active.

18.   b.   The second sequence is the correct one, according to Kübler-Ross.

19.   d.   All of the factors listed except for Down syndrome are associated with violence in young people.

11

Personality

Class and Text Notes

Personality: An individual's unique pattern of thoughts, feelings, and behaviors that persists over time and across situations.

1. Psychodynamic Theories

    A. Sigmund Freud

        •   How personality is structured

            -Id

            - Pleasure principle

            - Ego

            - Reality principle

            - Superego

            - Ego ideal

        •   Defense Mechanism

            - Denial

            - Repression

            - Projection

            - Identification

            - Regression

            - Intellectualization

            - Reaction Formation

            - Displacement

            - Sublimation

        •   How Personality Develops

            - libido

- fixation

- oral stage

- anal stage

- phallic stage

- Oedipus complex, Electra complex

- latency period

- genital stage

B.   Carl Jung

Enduring Issues: Universal Human Archetypes

- • Personal unconscious, collective unconscious

- • Archetypes

- • Persona

- • Anima, animus

- • Extrovert, introvert

- • Rational individuals, irrational individuals

C.   Alfred Adler

- • Compensation

- • Inferiority complex

D.   Karen Horney

Enduring Issues: Is Biology Destiny?

E.   Erik Erikson

F.   A Psychodynamic View of Jaylene Smith

G.   Evaluating Psychodynamic Theories

Thinking Critically: Psychoanalysis

2.   Humanistic Personality Theories

A.   Carl Rogers

- • Actualizing tendency

        •   Conditional positive regard, unconditional positive regard

    B.   A Humanistic View of Jaylene Smith

    C.   Evaluating Humanistic Theories

3.   Trait Theories

    A.   Development of Trait Theory

Enduring Issues: Is Personality Inherited?

    B.   The Big Five

        •   Are the Big Five Personality Traits Universal?

Thinking Critically: Cultural Universals

    C.   A Trait View of Jaylene Smith

    D.   Evaluating Trait Theories

On the Cutting Edge: The Genetic Basis of Personality Traits

Enduring Issues: How Stable is Personality Over Time?

4.   Cognitive-Social Learning Theories

    A.   Expectancies, Self-Efficacy, and Locus of Control

Enduring Issues: How Does Personality Interact with the Environment?

    B.   A Cognitive-Social Learning View of Jaylene Smith

    C.   Evaluating Cognitive-Social Learning Theories

5.   Personality Assessment

    A.   The Personal Interview

    B.   Direct Observation

    C.   Objective Tests

        •   Sixteen Personality Factor Questionnaire

        •   NEO-PI-R

        •   Minnesota Multiphasic Personality Inventory (MMPI-2)

    D.   Projective Tests

        •   Rorschach test

        •   Thematic Apperception Test (TAT)

Web Investigations
www.prenhall.com/morris

Chapter 11: Personality and Graphology

After reading this chapter, you should have a better idea of how and why psychologists assess personality. You recognize that personality assessment is an exacting enterprise in which a properly prepared psychologist uses reliable and valid instruments to better understand an individual s personality.

Sounds like a lot of work, doesn't it? In practice, it is. Personality assessment may take several hours or days of test taking, questionnaire-completion, behavioral observations, and face-to-face interviews. While this kind of assessment results in the best possible picture of an individual s personality, it is labor- and personnel-intensive. It also has the disadvantage of being so obvious that the individual knows that she or he is being assessed. Wouldn't it be great if simpler and subtler personality assessment techniques existed, so that employers, educators, and others could use them with an interest (legitimate or otherwise) in learning more about someone s personality?

Graphology, the analysis of the shape and spacing of the words and letters in your handwriting to assess and predict personality, may be such a tool. Indeed, belief in the validity of graphology is strong among non-psychologists (and perhaps, a few psychologists) because it may be the quick and unobtrusive measure of personality that many seek. Consider the success of books like *The Complete Idiot s Guide to Handwriting Analysis* and *Handwriting analysis: putting it to work for you*, the latter of which has sold over 50,000 copies! This *Web Investigation* will apply critical thinking to the issue of graphology.

To begin, go to the Morris Companion Web Site at the internet site indicated above, select chapter 11, and click on **Web Investigations**.

Web Investigation 1: Exploring Graphology Estimated time = 5 minutes
Web Investigation 2: Meaning and Metaphor Estimated time = 5 minutes
Web Investigation 3: Barnum Effect Estimated time = 10 minutes

Multiple Choice Pretest

This pretest will help you identify the topics in the chapter that are most difficult for you. By focusing your study time in those areas, you will see the greatest improvement.

1. _____ is defined as the characteristic pattern of thoughts, feelings, and behavior that is stable over time and distinguishes one person from another.
   a. Learning
   b. Personality
   c. Habit
   d. Trait

2. Personality is shaped by a motive for personal growth and reaching one's maximum potential, according to _____ theories.
   a. psychodynamic
   b. trait
   c. humanistic
   d. social-cognitive

3. Personality is the result of unconscious, often sexual, motivations and conflicts, according to _____ theories.
   a. psychodynamic
   b. trait
   c. humanistic
   d. social-cognitive

4. Personality is shaped by the ways people think about, act on, and respond to their environment, according to _____ theories.
   a. psychodynamic
   b. trait
   c. humanistic
   d. social-cognitive

5. The term "sexual instinct," according to Freud, refers to _____.
   a. childhood experience
   b. desire for any pleasure
   c. erotic sexuality
   d. personal unconscious

6. According to Freud, the unconscious urges seek expression through the _____.
   a. id
   b. superego
   c. ego
   d. persona

7. Which of the following is MOST likely to be true regarding Jaylene Smith, in the case study presented in your text?
   a. Her personality is the result of an unresolved Oedipal complex and fixation in the phallic stage of development.
   b. Her personality is the result of certain inborn traits such as determination and persistence.
   c. Her personality is a reflection of a complex interaction of inherited predispositions, life experiences, and learned behaviors.
   d. Her personality is a reflection of a discrepancy between her self-concept and her inborn capacities.

8. According to Freud, the reality principle is _____.
   a. the way in which the ego tries to delay satisfying the id's desires until it can do so safely and successfully
   b. the way in which the id tries to obtain immediate gratification and avoid pain
   c. the way in which the ego ideal established standards of what one would like to be
   d. the way in which young children instinctively seek self-actualization

9. The standard of perfection by which the superego judges the ego's actions is known as the _____, in Freud theory.
   a. ego-ideal
   b. conscience
   c. animus
   d. archetype

10. When our superego is dominant, _____.
    a. we are able to fully enjoy a normal life
    b. we do not have any guilt feelings
    c. our drives are not regulated
    d. our behavior is too tightly controlled

11. Jim is impulsive and emotional. His behavior is illogical and he feels little guilt for what he does. Freud would say John's _____ is the dominant part of his personality.
    a. id
    b. ego
    c. superego
    d. persona

12. Freud calls the energy generated by the sexual instinct the _____.
    a. pleasure principle
    b. libido
    c. abreaction
    d. reality principle

13. Freud would have viewed someone who is argumentative, hostile, and lacks self-confidence as probably fixated in the _____ stage.
    a. oral
    b. anal
    c. phallic
    d. genital

14. Jung's theory of personality describes a "mask" which people project as their public self. This mask is known as _____.
    a. anima
    b. ego
    c. shadow
    d. persona

15. Jung called the feminine side of the male personality the _____.
    a. anima
    b. ego
    c. shadow
    d. persona

Answers and Explanations to Multiple Choice Pretest

1.   b.   This item includes the classic definition of personality.

2.   c.   Humanistic theorists emphasize the motive for personal growth and development.

3.   a.   Psychodynamic theorists emphasize unconscious motives and processes.

4.   d.   Cognitive-social learning theorists emphasize the ways a person thinks about and acts on his/her environment.

5.   b.   Any desire for pleasure, according to Freud, is a manifestation of the sexual instinct.

6.   a.   The id seeks to express unconscious urges.

7.   c.   The case study in the text about Jaylene details a very complex combination of genetic and environmental factors in forming her personality

8.   a.   The reality principle is the ego's way to delay expression of the id's desires until it is safe and appropriate.

9.   a.   Ego-ideal serves as the standard of perfection for judging the ego's actions.

10.   d   The superego is overly controlled, which would result in a person not satisfying enough basic urges.

11.   a.   The id is impulsive and emotional.

12.   b.   The energy generated by the sexual instinct is referred to as the libido.

13.   a.   Argumentative and hostile tendencies are associated with oral fixation, in Freud's view.

14.   d.   Persona is the term Jung used to refer to the "mask" of personality.

15.   a.   The anima is the female side of the male personality, and the animus is the male side of the female personality.

Learning Objectives

After you have read and studied this chapter, you should be able to complete the following statements. Your exam is written based on these learning objectives.

1. Define personality.

2. Summarize the interaction of Freud's id, ego, and super- ego.

3. Identify Freud's five stages of psychosexual development.

4. Differentiate between the theories of Jung, Adler, and Horney.

5. Identify Erik Erikson's eight stages of personality development.

6. Explain object relations theories of personality.

7. Contrast Carl Rogers' humanistic theory with Freudian theory.

8. Explain trait theory.

9. Discuss one example of a trait theory.

10. Compare cognitive social-learning theories to early views of personality.

11. Describe the four basic tools psychologists use to measure personality.

12. List two objective tests to their uses. List the advantages and disadvantages of objective test.

13. Discuss the advantages of projective tests.

14. Explain how the Rorschach Test and the Thematic Apperception Test are administered.

Short Essay Questions

Write out your answers to the following eight essay questions to further your mastery of the topics.

1. Explain how each of the four major types of personality theories views personality.

_____

_____

_____

_____

_____

_____

_____

_____

_____

_____

_____

2. Describe the function of each part of Freud's structure of personality.

_____

_____

_____

_____

_____

_____

_____

_____

_____

_____

3. Describe Horney's theory of personality and contrast it to Freud's personality theory.

_____

_____

_____

_____

_____

_____

_____

_____

_____

_____

_____

_____

4. Identify Freud's psychosexual stages, when they occur, and the effects of problems occurring at each stage.

_____

_____

_____

_____

_____

_____

_____

_____

_____

_____

5.   Describe the role of archetypes in Carl Jung's personality theory.

_____

_____

_____

_____

_____

_____

_____

_____

_____

_____

_____

_____

6. Identify what Adler felt were the driving forces of personality and how his views changed over time.

_____

_____

_____

_____

_____

_____

_____

_____

7. List the stages of Erikson's theory of development in chronological order, and briefly explain the associated conflict.

_____

_____

_____

_____

_____

_____

_____

_____

_____

_____

_____

_____

_____

8. Compare and contrast the strengths and weaknesses of various measures of personality: the interview, observation, objective tests, and projective tests.

_____

_____

_____

_____

_____

_____

_____

_____

_____

_____

_____

Language Support

Students identified the following words from the text as needing more explanation. This page can be cut out, folded in half, and used as a bookmark for this chapter.

A

altercation	disagreement
ambiguous	not clear
amiable	friendly
attain	each

B

bickering	fighting

C

capture	include
coherent	logical and organized
conditional	depend on
conquering	winning
consensus	number of people who agree
constitutes	makes up, consists of
continuity	being continuous
cordial	polite

D

descriptors	something which explains a quality
disheartening	sad and discouraging
disposition	personality
drawbacks	problems

E

elicit	bring out
embodied	part of
emphasized	stressed as being important

evident	able to be seen

F

fate	what happens in a person's life
fosters	leads to

H

hallmark	of maturity important sign of maturity
hostility	anger

I

infer	conclude; reason
instances	times
intensified	got stronger
intuiting	to understand through getting a feeling about something

L

lofty	very high

M

maintain	keep
marine sergeant	a military officer in the marine corp.
mediocre	poor quality
millennia	1,000 years
misinterpret	get a wrong understanding of something
mysticism	spiritual approach

N

narcissism	to love oneself too much
nonessential	not necessary

O

one-dimensional	only one part

P

pessimistic	look at things in a negative (bad) way
pursue	go after
R	
recruits	low ranking soldiers
retaining	keeping in
rivalry	competition
S	
salient	important
self-restraint	control of oneself
shifted the focus	changed the main concern
T	
thrived	grew very well
U	
unique	unusual

Multiple Choice Posttest

After studying the text and completing the Study Guide activities, answer these questions to determine if you need to review any areas before the course exam.

1. Which of the following is NOT an aspect of personality?
    a. enduring
    b. unique
    c. stable
    d. unpredictable

2. _____ theories state that personality is shaped by a motive for personal growth and reaching one's maximum potential.
    a. Psychodynamic
    b. Trait
    c. Humanistic
    d. Social-cognitive

3. According to _____ theories, personality is the result of unconscious, often sexual, motivations and conflicts.
    a. psychodynamic
    b. trait
    c. humanistic
    d. social-cognitive

4. According to Freud, the unconscious urges seek expression through the _____.
    a. id
    b. ego
    c. superego
    d. persona

5. When our id is dominant, _____.
    a. we are able to fully enjoy a normal life
    b. we do not have any guilt feelings
    c. our drives are not regulated
    d. our behavior is too tightly controlled

6. Jung called the male side of the female personality the _____.
    a. anima
    b. animus
    c. shadow
    d. persona

7. Adler felt that a driving force in shaping personality was overcoming feelings of _____.
    a. basic anxiety
    b. inhibition
    c. inferiority
    d. individualism

8. In the Jaylene Smith case study in the text, Erikson's theory would see the root of her problem as her inability to establish a sense of _____.
    a. trust
    b. generativity
    c. autonomy
    d. identity

9. Carl Rogers theorized that people brought up with unconditional positive regard _____.
   a. are unlikely to be fully functioning
   b. tend to be vain and narcissistic
   c. live lives directed toward what others want and value
   d. feel valued

10. It appears that people tend to learn to perceive events in their lives optimistically or pessimistically _____.
    a. at an early age
    b. during college
    c. during young adulthood
    d. during middle age

11. A person's expectancies become a critical part of his or her _____, according to Bandura and Rotter.
    a. self-actualization
    b. explanatory style
    c. ideal self
    d. persona

12. When explaining personality, cognitive-social learning theorists put _____ at the center of personality.
    a. unconscious processes
    b. emotional stability
    c. mental processes
    d. environmental cues

13. The most widely used objective personality test is the _____.
    a. 16PF
    b. TAT
    c. Rorschach
    d. MMPI-2

14. A behaviorist would prefer _____ when assessing someone's personality.
    a. objective tests
    b. observation
    c. interviews
    d. projective tests

15. Psychodynamic theorists believe that objective tests are of little use because _____.
    a. they are usually not valid
    b. it is difficult to agree on the meaning of test results
    c. they are difficult to score
    d. people are not usually aware of the unconscious determinants of their behavior

16. The Rorschach test relies on the interpretation of _____ to understand personality.
    a. a 16 part questionnaire
    b. cards with human figures on them
    c. 10 cards containing ink blots
    d. sentence completion exercises

17. Each of the following characterizations is true of humanistic theories, *except*:
    a. they have been criticized as being too rosy
    b. they suffer from a lack of scientific evidence
    c. they emphasize the importance of past experiences
    d. they promote a view of the self that fosters self-centeredness

Answers to Multiple Choice Posttest

1.   d.   Because personality is stable, it is somewhat predictable.

2.   c.   Humanistic theories stress the motive for personal growth.

3.   a.   Psychodynamic theories emphasize the role of unconscious motives and conflicts.

4.   a.   The id is the means sought for expression of unconscious urges.

5.   c.   Our drives are not regulated when our id is dominant.

6.   b.   Animus, according to Jung, is the female side of personality.

7.   c.   Feelings of inferiority is the driving force shaping personality, according to Adler.

8.   a.   Erikson's theory would view Jaylene Smith's difficulties as being due to her inability to establish a sense of trust.

9.   d.   If we were brought up with unconditional positive regard, we feel valued.

10.   a.   We learn to have either an optimistic or pessimistic view of the world very early in life.

11.   b.   Explanatory style is based much on one's expectancies.

12.   c.   Cognitive-social learning theorists emphasize mental processes.

13.   d.   The MMPI-2 is the most widely used objective measure of personality.

14.   b.   Behaviorists emphasize the importance of direct observation of behavior.

15.   d.   Psychodynamic theorists doubt the utility of objective tests of personality because they claim people lack insight into the true underlying causes of their behavior.

16.   c.   Rorschach uses cards with ink blots.

17.   c.   Humanistic theories are optimistic and future-oriented.

12

Stress and Health Psychology

Class and Text Notes

Stress   A state of psychological tension or strain.

Stressors   The events or circumstances that trigger stress.

1.   Sources of Stress

     A.   Life Changes

          •   Social Readjustment Rating Scale -- SRRS (Holmes and Rahe)

     B.   Everyday Hassles

          •   Pressure

          •   Frustration

Thinking Critically: Road Rage and You

     C.   Conflict

          -   Approach/approach conflict

          -   Avoidance/avoidance conflict

          -   Approach/avoidance conflict

     C.   Stress and Individual Differences

          •   Hardiness and Resilience

          •   Self-imposed Stress

2.   Coping with Stress

     A.   Direct Coping

          •   Confrontation

          •   Compromise

          •   Withdrawal

     B.   Defensive Coping

Enduring Issues: Coping Strategies

223

C.   Socioeconomic and Gender Differences

On the Cutting Edge: "Tend and Befriend": A Female Response to Stress?

3.   Stress and Health

    A.   The Biology of Stress

Enduring Issues: Psychological Stress and Physical Illness

Thinking Critically: "Genes Lie Behind Only About 30% of Cancers Studied"

    B.   Stress and Heart Disease

        •   Type A; Type B

    C.   Stress and the Immune System

        •   Psychoneuroimmunology

4.   Staying Healthy

    A.   Methods of Reducing Stress

        •   Calm Down

        •   Reach Out

        •   Religion and Altruism

        •   Learn to Cope Effectively

        •   Coping with Stress at College

    B.   Adopt A Healthy Lifestyle

        •   Diet

        •   Exercise

        •   Quit Smoking

        •   Avoid High Risk Behaviors

5.   Extreme Stress

    A.   Sources of Extreme Stress

        •   Unemployment and Underemployment

        •   Divorce and separation

        •   Bereavement

        •   Catastrophes

- Combat and Other Threatening Personal Attacks

B. Post-Traumatic Stress Disorder

6. The Well-Adjusted Person

Thinking Critically: Who Is Well Adjusted?

Specific criteria to evaluate adjustment:

A. Does the action meet the demand? or just postpone?

B. Does the action meet the individual's needs?

C. Is the action compatible with the well-being of others?

Web Investigations
www.prenhall.com/morris

Chapter 12: Investigating Gangs and Behavior

You might not immediately think of gangs as a health issue, yet most medical authorities note that behavioral factors, such as poor diet, lack of exercise, addictive behaviors, and unsafe acts, are major *preventable* sources of illness in our society. Certainly gangs promote several of these unhealthy factors, including addiction and risky criminal conduct. Gangs use violence to defend their territories, commit revenge on rival groups, and to keep wayward members in line with the group's authority. Often, these practices involve handguns with lethal consequences. Moreover, gangs represent a significant source of stress for members of a community who are subjected to their presence. Clearly, ours would be a healthier society that would enjoy a higher quality of life without the deleterious influence of gangs.

But gangs exist for reasons beyond the illegal and unhealthy behaviors they frequently promote. Understanding why individuals join gangs is at the core of efforts to prevent gangs or to reduce their influence. This *Web Investigation* provides an overview of the functions and activities of gangs.

To begin, go to the Morris Companion Web Site at the internet address shown above, select chapter 12, and click on **Web Investigations**

Multiple Choice Pretest

This pretest will help you identify the topics in the chapter that are most difficult for you. By focusing your study time in those areas, you will see the greatest improvement.

1. _____ psychology is a subfield concerned with the relationship between psychological factors and physical health or illness.
   a.   Forensic
   b.   Neuroimmunology
   c.   Environmental
   d.   Health

2. A demand that leads to a state of tension or threat and requires change is called _____.
   a.   pressure
   b.   stress
   c.   adjustment
   d.   arousal

3. The Social Readjustment Rating Scale measures _____.
   a.   the degree to which one has resolved stress
   b.   family situations
   c.   the degree to which flexibility is genetically determined
   d.   how much stress a person has undergone in a given period

4. You are having a difficult time deciding whether to vacation in Hawaii or Tahiti. This type of conflict is called _____.
   a.   avoidance/avoidance
   b.   approach/approach
   c.   avoidance/approach
   d.   approach/avoidance

5. Albert Ellis described an internal source of stress due to _____.
   a.   hardiness traits
   b.   faulty response cues
   c.   faulty expectations
   d.   irrational beliefs

6. An effective way of coping with a conflict is to _____.
   a.   deny the conflict   c. be aggressive
   b.   withdraw   d. compromise

7. Freud believed that people use self-deceptive techniques for reducing stress that are called _____.
   a.   avoidance behavior
   b.   regressive syndrome
   c.   maladaptive behavior
   d.   defense mechanisms

8. Everyday hassles include all of the following *except*:
   a.   a petty argument with a friend
   b.   a broken zipper
   c.   deciding to divorce
   d.   having to wait in a long line

9. Professor James recommends a relatively simple technique to help people see their own tendencies toward road rage. What is it?
   a. sit quietly and meditate in their car while it is parked
   b. tape record their thoughts while they drive
   c. request a copy of their driving record and then review it carefully
   d. wear a mask so that they will not be identifiable while driving

10. Being "caught between a rock and a hard place" is very much like what type of conflict discussed in the text?.
   a. approach/approach
   b. approach/avoidance
   c. avoidance/avoidance
   d. none of these

11. Utilizing a defense mechanism becomes maladaptive when _____.
   a. it leads to superstitious behavior
   b. it protects feelings of self-worth
   c. it interferes with a person's ability to function
   d. people use it a lot

12. Selye describes the General Adaptation Syndrome as proceeding in the following order:
   a. resistance, alarm reaction, exhaustion
   b. alarm reaction, resistance, exhaustion
   c. exhaustion, resistance, alarm reaction
   d. resistance, alarm reaction, exhaustion

13. People who respond to life events in an easy going way are exhibiting a _____ behavior pattern.
   a. Type A
   b. Type B
   c. Type E
   d. Type S

14. Which of the following correctly lists the order of reaction to catastrophes?
   a. confusion, rage, recovery
   b. rage, confusion, recovery
   c. suggestible stage, shock stage, recovery stage
   d. shock stage, suggestible stage, recovery stage

15. For someone to heal from posttraumatic disorder depends a great deal on _____.
   a. how much emotional support the victim gets from family, friends, and community
   b. whether the person experienced the stressful event alone, or with others
   c. whether the victim is a male or a female
   d. whether the person has an internal or external locus of control

16. Maslow's theory states that individuals who are well-adjusted attempt to _____.
   a. remain aloof from the rest of society
   b. convince others that they have no faults
   c. actualize themselves
   d. win others to their way of thinking

17. Research done by Taylor found that mentally healthy people _____ their ability to control chance events and believe that the future will be _____ than the present.
   a. underestimate; worse
   b. accurately estimate; the same
   c. overestimate; better
   d. overestimate; worse

Answers and Explanations to Multiple Choice Pretest

1. d. Health psychology is concerned with links between psychological factors and physical health or illness

2. b. Stress is a demand that leads to a state of tension that requires a change.

3. d. The SRS measures amount of stress experienced in a given time period.

4. b. Deciding between two good alternatives is called an approach/approach conflict.

5. d. Ellis stressed the importance of irrational beliefs as causes of stress.

6. d. Compromise is often an effective way to cope with conflict.

7. d. Freud emphasized the importance of defense mechanisms for reducing stress.

8. c. Divorce is a major life change, not a mere daily hassle.

9. b. The recommendation is to tape record one's thoughts while driving.

10. c. Being "caught between a rock and a hard place" is much like an avoidance/avoidance conflict—having to choose between two undesirable options.

11. c. Defense mechanisms help us deal with anxiety but they can interfere with normal functioning.

12. b. The correct order is alarm reaction, resistance, and then exhaustion.

13. b. Type B pattern is associated with an easy going response style to life events.

14. d. The correct order is shock, suggestible, and then recovery.

15. a. Support from family, friends, and community is important to someone trying to heal from PTSD.

16. c. Well-adjusted persons attempt to actualize themselves, according to Maslow.

17. c. Taylor found that mentally healthy people overestimate their ability to control events and are optimistic about the future.

Learning Objectives

After you have read and studied this chapter, you should be able to complete the following statements. Your exam is written based on learning objectives similar to these.

1. Define adjustment and stress. Identify sources of stress.

2. Describe the nature of pressure, frustration, conflict, anxiety, and identify situations that produce each one.

3. Identify the five basic sources of frustration.

4. Give examples of each of the following: approach/approach conflict; avoidance/avoidance conflict; approach/avoidance conflict; double approach/avoidance conflict.

5. Distinguish between direct coping and defensive coping.

6. Identify and characterize the three ways that people cope directly.

7. Describe all of the defense mechanisms.

8. Discuss the psychological and physiological effects of stress on people.

9. Identify five sources of extreme stress.

10. Discuss the opposing views of what characterizes a well- adjusted individual.

Short Essay Questions

Write out your answers to the following four essay questions to further your mastery of the topics.

1. Describe various types of stressors and discuss how they relate to stress.

_____

_____

_____

_____

_____

_____

_____

_____

_____

_____

_____

_____

2. Describe three direct coping methods contrast them with defensive coping.

_____

_____

_____

_____

_____

_____

_____

_____

_____

_____

_____

_____

3. Outline the General Adaptation Syndrome (GAS) model.

_____

_____

_____

_____

_____

_____

_____

_____

_____

_____

_____

_____

_____

4. Describe how stress affects the immune system.

_____

_____

_____

_____

_____

_____

_____

_____

_____

_____

_____

_____

232

5. List and briefly describe several methods of reducing stress.

_____

_____

_____

_____

_____

_____

_____

_____

_____

_____

4. Discuss post-traumatic stress disorder. Describe how positive growth might result from significant personal trauma.

_____

_____

_____

_____

_____

_____

_____

_____

_____

_____

Language Support

Students identified the following words from the text as needing more explanation. This page can be cut out, folded in half, and used as a bookmark for this chapter.

A

alleviating	getting rid of
ambivalent	not to care
annoyance	something that bothers us
apathetic	do not care

B

baseball runner	a person who is running to a base in the game of baseball

C

captors	persons holding hostages
cherish	enjoy a lot
chronic	keeps happening; long-lasting
collapse	fall
compelled	forced or pressured to do something
component	part
controversy	disagreement
conventionally	like most other people do it
conversely	on the other hand; also
coupled with	together with
custodial parent	parent with whom children live

D

debating team	a team at school that practices speaking for or against topics
desperate	frantic; last try
dilemma	problem
disastrous	very bad
dissecting	cutting apart

E

endured	lived through
exhausting	very tiring
exploding in rage	violent anger
extravagantly	an extreme amount

F

fatigue	being tired
forbidden	are not allowed to do

G

girder	a beam used to make some buildings
gracious	giving and kind

H

hardship	difficulty in life
hallmark	key feature
hostage	someone held against their will by criminals

L

looms	stands in the way

M

mobilize	to get together

O

obstacle	something you have to get over
overly optimistic	see only the good side of something when they should also be seeing the bad side

P

perched	sitting on top of
procrastination	put things off until later

Q

quarantined	put away; confined

R

relentless	always present; never-ending
resilient	remain strong
restraint	calm behavior
rid	eliminate
ruminate	keep worrying about
ruthless	not caring if others are hurt

S

self-assurance	good feelings about ability
survivors	people who live through something bad

T

thrive	do very well
trivial	small and not important

U

ubiquitous	everywhere
unrealistic	not possible
utterly	totally

V

vacillation	changing back and forth

Multiple Choice Posttest

After studying the text and completing the Study Guide activities, answer these questions to determine if you need to review any areas before the course exam.

1. Hardiness is a trait in which _____.
   a. authoritative parenting has led to greater levels of resistance to stress
   b. our experience of stress is affected by heredity
   c. people experience difficult environmental demands as challenging rather than threatening
   d. people react to conflict in a hard way

2. Deciding on a more realistic solution to a problem when an ideal solution does not seem to be possible is called _____.
   a. confrontation
   b. withdrawal
   c. aggression
   d. compromise

3. Using withdrawal as a way of coping may create future problems in that it will _____.
   a. result in denial
   b. result in avoidance of similar future situations
   c. result in aggressive actions
   d. eliminate the chance for future compromise

4. _____ people are able to "bounce back" and regain self-confidence and a hopeful attitude after extreme or prolonged stress.
   a. Resilient
   b. Adverse
   c. Compromisers
   d. Type A

5. A woman copes with the frustration of not being promoted despite many years of hard work on the job by trying persuade her boss that she is ready to handle a better job at the company headquarters. This type of coping is an example of _____.
   a. confrontation
   b. compromise
   c. withdrawal
   d. self-deception

6. People exhibit _____ when they express exaggerated emotions and ideas that are the opposite of their real emotions.
   a. reaction formation
   b. intellectualization
   c. repression
   d. displacement

7. You get yelled at by your boss and come home and yell at your roommate. You are using the defense mechanism of _____.
   a. reaction formation
   b. intellectualization
   c. repression
   d. displacement

8. Defense mechanisms are used by all people; however, they become a problem when they _____.
   a. lead to superstitious behavior
   b. interfere with a person's ability to function
   c. protect feelings of self-worth
   d. are used too much

9. A coping strategy that seems to be much more characteristic of females than males is:
   a. aggression
   b. resorting to alcohol
   c. "tend and befriend"
   d. confrontation

10. The key aspects of the Type A behavior pattern for the link to coronary heart disease seem to be:
    a. impaired immune system functioning
    b. chronic anger and hostility
    c. selfishness
    d. guilt

11. People who respond to life events in an intense, time urgent manner are exhibiting a _____ behavior pattern.
    a. Type A   c. Type E
    b. Type B   d. Type S

12. The incidence of _____ has been shown to increase in mice that are exposed to stressful noise.
    a. hypertension
    b. heart disease
    c. stomach ulcers
    d. cancer

13. A person's first reaction to a disaster is _____.
    a. despair
    b. confusion
    c. shock
    d. anger

14. When stressful events in the past result in anxiety, sleeplessness, and nightmares, a psychological disorder called _____ might be occurring.
    a. generalized anxiety disorder
    b. panic disorder
    c. posttraumatic stress disorder
    e. narcoleptic disorder

15. When people are well-adjusted they probably have _____.
    a. learned to get what they need regardless of what others want
    b. learned to balance conformity and nonconformity as well as self-control and spontaneity
    c. few problems
    d. none of the above

16. All of the following criteria are listed in the text as ways of evaluating adjustment EXCEPT _____.
    a. Does the action meet the individual's needs?
    b. Does the action meet the demand to adjust or does it simply postpone resolving the problem?
    c. Does the action conform to society's norms?
    d. Is the action compatible with the well-being of others?

Answers and Explanations to Multiple Choice Posttest

1.   c.   Hardy persons experience demands as challenging rather than threatening.
2.   d.   Compromise entails opting for a reasonable solution over an unlikely ideal one.
3.   b.   Withdrawal can lead to future avoidance in similar situations
4.   a.   Resilient people can "bounce back" from adversity.
5.   a.   Attempting to change her bosses view entails confrontation.
6.   a.   Reaction formation is the expression of exaggerated emotions that are opposite the true emotions.
7.   d.   Displacement is taking your anger out on someone other than the person who made you angry.
8.   b.   Defense mechanisms are a problem when then interfere with one's ability to function.
9.   c.   Females use the "tend and befriend" strategy more than do males.
10.   b.   Chronic anger and hostility are especially associated with CHD.
11.   a.   Type A behavior pattern involves intensity and time urgency.
12.   d.   Exposure of stressful noise has been associated with cancer in rats.
13.   c.   Shock is typically the first reaction to a disaster.
14.   c.   PTSD entails re-experiencing the stress (anxiety, sleeplessness, nightmares) associated with past stressful events.
15.   b.   Well-adjusted persons are better at achieving balance in their lives.
16.   c.   Conformity to society's norms is not a critical feature of adjustment.

13

Psychological Disorders

Class and Text Notes

1. Perspectives on Psychological Disorders

   - Society

   - Individual

   - Mental-health Professional

   A. Historical Views of Psychological Disorders

   B. Theories of the Nature, Causes, and Treatment of Psychological Disorders

      - The Biological Model

      - The Psychoanalytic Model

      - The Cognitive-Behavioral Model

      - The Diathesis-Stress Model and Systems Theory

   Enduring Issues: Causes of Mental disorders

   C. Classifying Psychological Disorders

      - Diagnostic and Statistical Manual of Mental Disorders (DSM-V)

   D. The Prevalence of Psychological Disorders

   E. Mental Illness and the Law

2. Mood Disorders

   A. Depression

   B. Mania and Bipolar Disorder

   Applying Psychology: Recognizing Depression

   C. Causes of Mood Disorders

      - Biological factors

      - Psychological factors

      - Social factors

241

7.   Personality Disorders

    A.   Types of Personality Disorders

- Schizoid Personality Disorder

- Paranoid Personality Disorder

- Dependent Personality Disorder

- Avoidant Personality Disorder

- Narcissistic Personality Disorder

- Borderline Personality Disorder

- Antisocial Personality Disorder

    B.   Causes of Personality Disorder

Thinking Critically: Causation

8.   Schizophrenic Disorders

- Hallucinations

- Delusions

    A.   Types of Schizophrenic Disorders

- Disorganized Schizophrenia

- Catatonic Schizophrenia

- Paranoid Schizophrenia

- Undifferentiated Schizophrenia

    B.   Causes of Schizophrenia

Thinking Critically: Genius and Mental Disorders

9.   Childhood Disorders

    A.   Attention-deficit/Hyperactivity Disorder (AD/HD)

       - Psychostimulants

Thinking Critically: AD/HD

    B.   Autistic Disorder

10.   Gender and Cultural Differences in Psychological Disorders

    A.   Gender Differences

B.   Cultural differences

Enduring Issues: Are We All Alike?

Web Investigations
www.prenhall.com/morris

Chapter 13: Recognizing Mood Disorders

Everyone experiences some mood changes. While life presents its share of ups and downs to all of us, some people experience sufficient problems with moods that professional attention is warranted. As noted in this chapter, problems for which a professional may be indicated generally include maladaptive behavior that interferes with our functioning in life, serious subjective discomfort, or both. While extreme cases are always the most easily judged and diagnosed, applying the correct diagnostic label is not as easy for disorders that share similar features but have different causes and courses and respond differently to treatment. Moreover, the act of providing a diagnostic label has serious consequences for how a labeled individual is viewed by professionals and others, making diagnosis a skill best left to those with adequate education and experience.

Understanding what a psychologist or other professional would view as abnormal, then, aids our appreciation of the diagnostic process and should caution us against the casual labeling of others or ourselves. This *Web Investigation* will give you some samples of abnormal behavior related to moods and permit you to apply your perspective in diagnosing mood disorders.

To begin, go to the Morris Companion Web Site at the internet address shown above, select chapter 13, and click on **Web Investigations**. Spend some time learning about how to recognize mood disorders.

Multiple Choice Pretest

This pretest will help you identify the topics in the chapter that are most difficult for you. By focusing your study time in those areas, you will see the greatest improvement.

1. Which of the following statements is true?
    a. In recent years, psychologists and mental-health professionals have been able to arrive at a single definition of normal or abnormal behavior.
    b. The mental-health professional's concern is whether the individual's behavior con forms to the existing social order.
    c. Defining behavior as normal or abnormal depends on whose standards values are used.
    d. The definitions of normal or abnormal behavior must come from the mental-health profession.

2. The _____ view of mental illness dominated nearly all early societies.
    a. psychological
    b. naturalistic
    c. philosophical
    d. supernatural

3. During the Middle Ages many people believed psychological disorders resulted from supernatural forces and that the treatment of choice was _____.
    a. exorcism
    b. herbal cures
    c. purging with leeches
    d. magic potions

4. Early asylums were _____.
    a. primitive, but using relatively effective treatment
    b. places of human care, although they had no formal methods of treating mental illness
    c. reserved only for the rich who were mentally ill
    d. basically prisons

5. The _____ explanation of mental illness states that psychological disorders are caused by physical malfunction that can sometimes be genetic.
    a. psychodynamic
    b. biological
    c. naturalistic
    d. cognitive-behavioral

6. The _____ model of mental illness states that psychological disorders are caused by unconscious conflicts.
    a. psychoanalytic
    b. biological
    c. naturalistic
    d. cognitive-behavioral

7. Sarah has an extreme fear of public speaking that is interfering with her job. Her psychologist believes that the fear is learned and can be unlearned with appropriate reinforcement. This view is typical of the _____ model.
    a. psychodynamic
    b. biological
    c. naturalistic
    d. behavioral

8. Elaina is very depressed and has self-defeating beliefs. Her therapist states that her depression is caused by her negative thinking. This view is typical of the _____ model.
    a. biological
    b. cognitive
    c. behavioral
    d. psychoanalytic

9. The view that heart disease results from a combination of genetic predisposition, stress, certain personality styles, poor health behaviors, and competitive pressure is typical of the _____ approach to abnormal behavior.
    a. multimodal
    b. psychoneuroimmunological
    c. eclectic
    d. systems

10. Diathesis is thought to be a _____.
    a. split personality
    b. mental weakness
    c. physical disability
    d. biological predisposition

11. Mental disorders are categorized according to _____ in the DSM-V .
    a. family histories
    b. biological cause of disruptive behavior
    c. significant behavior patterns
    d. specific theoretical approaches

12. Psychologists use the term "affect" to refer to _____.
    a. emotion
    b. intuition
    c. thought
    d. behavior

13. When people are _____ they have lost touch with reality.
    a. manic
    b. neurotic
    c. psychotic
    d. psychopathic

14. The symptoms of _____ include excessive excitement, fast speech followed by times of extreme sadness.
    a. dysthymia
    b. mania
    c. bipolar disorder
    d. conversion disorder

15. Eileen has an intense fear of airplanes. She is probably experiencing a _____ disorder.
    a. panic
    b. generalized anxiety
    c. conversion
    d. phobic

16. The disorder previously known as "multiple personality disorder" is now known as
    _____.
    a. dissociative amnesia
    b. dissociative identity disorder
    c. dissociative fugue
    d. depersonalization disorder

17. Which diagnostic category includes disorders that involve actual physical ailments caused by psychological factors such as stress?
    a. body dysmorphic disorder
    b. hypochrondiasis
    c. dissociative fugue
    d. psychosomatic disorders

Answers to Multiple Choice Pretest

1.   c.   Various perspectives are available; each reflects different standards and values.

2.   d.   Early societies tended to accept the supernatural view of mental illness.

3.   a.   During the Middle Ages, exorcism was often the treatment of choice for mental illness.

4.   d.   Early asylums were basically prisons.

5.   b.   The biological perspective sees mental illnesses as being caused by physical malfunction.

6.   a.   The psychoanalytic model emphasizes unconscious conflict in mental illness.

7.   d.   Behaviorists believe that maladaptive behaviors are learned and that they can be unlearned.

8.   b.   Negative thinking as a cause of depression is consistent with the cognitive model.

9.   d.   The systems approach emphasizes these various contributions to disease.

10.   d.   Diathesis is thought to be a biological predisposition.

11.   c.   The DSM-V relies heavily on significant behavior patterns for categorizing disorders.

12.   a.   "Affect" is synonymous with emotion.

13.   c.   Having lost contact with reality is referred to as psychosis.

14.   c.   Bipolar disorder involves both manic and depressive aspects.

15.   d.   Fear of airplanes is an example of a phobia.

16.   b.   The current term for "multiple personality disorder" is dissociative identity disorder.

17.   d.   Psychosomatic disorders involve physical symptoms caused by psychological factors.

Learning Objectives

After you have read and studied this chapter, you should be able to complete the following statements. Your exam is likely to be largely based on these learning objectives.

1. Distinguish among the standards for defining psychological disorders from the view of society, the individual, and the mental-health professional.

2. Summarize historical attitudes toward psychological disorders.

3. State the four current models of psychological disorders and explain the diasthesis-stress model.

4. Explain how the DSM-V classifies mental disorders.

5. Distinguish between the two basic kinds of affective disorders and how they may interact with each other.

6. Describe and compare the anxiety disorder.

7. Recognize the characteristics of the psychophysiological disorders and the somatoform disorders.

8. Characterize three different types of dissociative disorders.

9. Define and give examples of the sexual disorders.

10. Define gender-identity disorders.

11. Define personality disorders. Describe four kinds of personality disorders.

12. Describe four types of schizophrenic disorders and identify possible causes of the disorder.

13. List characteristics of children with attention-deficit/ hyperactivity disorder.

Short Essay Questions

Write out your answers to the following essay questions to further your mastery of the topics.

1.   Is the insanity defense ever valid?

_____

_____

_____

_____

_____

_____

_____

_____

_____

_____

_____

2.   Compare and contrast four current views of psychological disorders.

_____

_____

_____

_____

_____

_____

_____

_____

_____

_____

_____

_____

3. Describe the symptoms and causes of psychosomatic disorders.

_____

_____

_____

_____

_____

_____

_____

_____

_____

_____

_____

_____

_____

4. Summarize current efforts to classify psychological disorders.

_____

_____

_____

_____

_____

_____

_____

_____

_____

_____

_____

5. Compare and contrast simple phobias, social phobias, and agoraphobia.

_____

_____

_____

_____

_____

_____

_____

_____

_____

_____

_____

_____

_____

6. Define gender-identity and summarize the research regarding its development.

_____

_____

_____

_____

_____

_____

_____

_____

_____

_____

_____

_____

7. Discuss three different types of sexual dysfunction.

_____

_____

_____

_____

_____

_____

_____

_____

_____

_____

_____

_____

_____

8. Explain what is known about attention-deficit hyperactivity disorder.

_____

_____

_____

_____

_____

_____

_____

_____

_____

_____

_____

Language Support

Students identified the following words from the text as needing more explanation. This page can be cut out, folded in half, and used as a bookmark for this chapter.

A

apathetic	not caring
appealing	interesting, likable
apprehensiveness	worried that something bad is going to happen
arbitrary	uncertain, changeable

B

bizarre	odd, very unusual
blithe	cheerful
bolster	build up
brilliant	very smart

C

captured	got
causative	that which causes
chiefly	mainly
cluster	group
coexist	to be at the same time
comprehensive	complete and thorough
considerable	a lot
criterion	standard
cynicism	doubt

D

debilitating	destructive; interfering
dismaying	upsetting
disobedient	not following rules
disparaging	negative

254

distinct	separate
dubious	questionable

E

eccentric	very unusual; odd
emerged	came out
enduring	lasting
entitlement	supposed to have
essential	very important
euphoria	feeling very good
exemplifies	is an example of
exhaustion	being very tired
exhibit	show
exhilarated	very happy
exploit	take advantage of unfairly

F

facsimiles	to look similar to
faked	pretend
fanciful	not serious
forbidden	not allowed
fruitfully	successfully
full-blown	fully

G

genuinely	truly
grimacing	facial expression of pain

H

horrifying	very bad
humiliating	very embarrassing
hypervigilance	too alert

I

ideology	organized ideas
impairment	does not work right
impassive	won't move
inadequate	not enough
incoherence	not able to be understood
incompetence	not skilled
incomprehensible	cannot be understood
inner distress	feel bad inside
intended	meant to be
invulnerable	cannot be hurt

J

jittery	nervous

L

legitimate	real

M

maladaptive	does not work
mannerisms	facial expressions and body movements
melancholy	sad
momentum	energy; movement

N

nurture	environmental influence

O

obliged	forced to

P

painstakingly	very carefully
paralyzing	so strong that you can't move
plagued with	having a problem with

potpourri	mixture of many different types
promiscuity	having sexual relationships which are outside of cultural norms

R

readily	easily
recurrence	happens again
resurface	come out again
reverted	went back to
rival	gang group of young people who are against the other group

S

scaffolding	boards and braces that workers stand on to build things high in the air
scarcity	not enough
shed some light on	explain
skeptical	having doubt about something
social deviance	not acting the way society think they should
spectrum	range
stew	think about and be upset
subtle	not obvious, small
sweeping conclusions	broad decisions

T

territory	area
timid	shy
trivial	small and not important
tyrannical	not fair, very controlling

U

unconventional	not usual
unrealistically	not with what is real

V

vindictiveness	wanting to get back at people

vital	very important
W	
wrenching	very painful

Multiple Choice Posttest

After studying the text and completing the Study Guide activities, answer these questions to determine if you need to review any areas before the course exam.

1. Which of the following is NOT a sexual disorder listed by the DSM-V?
   a. sexual dysfunction
   b. paraphilias
   c. gender identity disorder
   d. sexual orientation disorder

2. All of the following are paraphilias EXCEPT _____.
   a. exhibitionism
   b. pedophilia
   c. vaginismus
   d. sadomasochism

3. A disorder called _____ consists of wearing clothing of the opposite sex for sexual excitement and gratification.
   a. exhibitionism
   b. pedophilia
   c. transvestism
   d. sadomasochism

4. Causing humiliation or physical harm to sexual partners is characteristic of _____.
   a. exhibitionism
   b. pedophilia
   c. vaginismus
   d. sadists

5. A person who feels trapped in his or her body and since childhood pictures themselves as the other gender has a disorder called _____.
   a. gender identity disorder
   b. transvestism
   b. hermaphroditism
   d. sexual orientation disorder

6. A person who seems withdrawn, unfeeling and distant would probably be diagnosed with a(n) _____personality disorder.
   a. narcissistic
   b. schizoid
   c. paranoid
   d. antisocial

7. _____ disorders are inflexible and maladaptive ways of thinking and acting that are so exaggerated that they cause serious distress and social problems.
   a. Somatoform
   b. Manic
   c. Affective
   d. Personality

8. Nicole thinks of herself as extremely beautiful and intelligent. She always wants to be the center of attention. Nicole probably has a _____ personality.
   a. histrionic
   b. paranoid
   c. schizoid
   d. narcissistic

9. A personality disorder characterized by marked instability in self-image, mood, and interpersonal relationships is _____ personality disorder.
   a. borderline
   b. narcissistic
   c. antisocial
   d. schizoid

10. People exhibiting a(n) _____ personality disorder lie, steal, show no sense of responsibility, and no guilt for their behavior.
   a. borderline
   b. schizoid
   c. antisocial
   d. paranoid

11. A research study indicated that _____ percent of the populations in two prisons are antisocial personalities.
   a. 25
   b. 50
   c. 60
   d. 80

12. Disorders of inappropriate emotions, bizarre behaviors and thoughts are called _____.
   a. sexual dysfunctions
   b. dissociative
   c. somatoform
   d. schizophrenic

13. Severe problems of motor activity is a primary feature of _____ schizophrenia.
   a. disorganized
   b. undifferentiated
   c. catatonic
   d. paranoid

14. Extreme suspiciousness is seen in _____ schizophrenia.
   a. disorganized
   b. undifferentiated
   c. catatonic
   d. paranoid

15. Excessive amounts of the neurotransmitter _____ may increase a person's predisposition to schizophrenia.
   a. serotonin
   b. norepinephrine
   c. dopamine
   d. acetylcholine

16. Mark is in constant motion and very easily distracted. He probably has _____.
    a. dysmorphic disorder
    b. attention-deficit hyperactivity disorder
    c. childhood autism
    d. reticular formation developmental disorder

17. _____ psychiatrists interview defendents in court to determine if they are mentally fit to stand trial.
    a. Prosecuint
    b. Diagnostic
    c. Developmental
    d. Forensic

18. People considering suicide usually feel very _____.
    a. bitter
    b. apathy
    c. hopeless
    d. dissociated

19. Which match between disorder and symptom is incorrect?
    a. autism - echolalia
    b. schizophrenia - delusions
    c. transvestic fetishism - cross-dressing
    d. body dysmorphic disorder - hallucinations

Answers and Explanations to Multiple Choice Posttest

1. d. Sexual orientation is not included as a sexual disorder in DSM-V.

2. c. Vaginismus is not a paraphilia, it is a sexual dysfunction.

3. c. Transvestites wear the clothing of the opposite sex.

4. d. Sadism is humiliating or harming others for sexual gratification.

5. a. Gender identity disorder patients feel trapped in the body of the opposite sex.

6. b. Schizoid personality disorder patients are withdrawn and distant.

7. d. Personality disorders entail exaggerated ways maladaptive ways of thinking, feeling and acting.

8. d. Nicole is described as narcissistic—with a greatly inflated sense of herself.

9. a. Borderline personality disorder entails a marked instability in self-image, mood, and interpersonal relationships.

10. c. Antisocial personalities show no guilt or sense of responsibility for their behaviors.

11. b. About half (50%) of inmates are likely antisocial personalities.

12. d. Schizophrenia entails bizarre behaviors and thoughts, as well as inappropriate emotions.

13. c. Catatonic schizophrenics exhibit severe motor disturbances.

14. d. Paranoid schizophrenics exhibit extreme suspiciousness.

15. c. Dopamine has been implicated in schizophrenia.

16. b. AD/HD entails poor attention and distractibility as well as constant moving.

17. d. Forensic psychologists work with the legal system.

18. c. Extreme hopelessness often precedes suicide.

19. d. Body dysmorphic disorder does not entail hallucinations.

14

THERAPIES

Class and Text Notes

1. Insight Therapies

    A. Psychoanalysis

        •   Free association

        •   Transference

        •   Insight

    B. Client-Centered Therapy

    C. Gestalt Therapy

    D. Recent Developments

        •   Short-term psychodynamic psychotherapy

On the Cutting Edge: Virtual Therapy

3. Behavior Therapies

    A. Using Classical Conditioning Techniques

        •   Desensitization, Extinction, Flooding

        •   Aversive conditioning

    B. Operant Conditioning

        •   Behavior contracting

        •   Token economy

    C. Modeling

4. Cognitive Therapies

    A. Stress-Inoculation Therapy

    B. Rational-Emotive Therapy

    C. Beck's Cognitive Therapy

4. Group Therapies

A.   Family Therapy

B.   Couple Therapy

C.   Self-Help Groups

5.   Effectiveness of Psychotherapy

- Does Psychotherapy Work?

Thinking Critically: Survey Results

- Which type of therapy is best for which disorder?

Applying Psychology: How to Find Help

6.   Biological Treatments

A.   Drug Therapies

- Antipsychotic drugs

- Antidepressant drugs

- Lithium

- Other medications

Enduring Issues: Combining Drugs and Psychotherapy

B.   Electroconvulsive Therapy

C.   Psychosurgery

Summary Table: Major Perspectives on Therapy

7.   Institutionalization and Its Alternatives

A.   Deinstitutionalization

B.   Alternative Forms of Treatment

C.   Prevention

- Primary prevention

- Secondary prevention

- Tertiary prevention

9.   Gender and Cultural Differences in Treatments

Thinking Critically: Access to Mental Health Care

Enduring Issues: On Being Culture Bound

Web Investigations

www.prenhall.com/morris

Chapter 14: Investigating Sex Differences in Depression

As you read in this chapter, significant gender differences exist in the prevalence of some psychological disorders. These gender differences extend to the treatment of disorders as well. Women, for example, are more likely to seek and obtain therapy. This might be the result of a society that views therapy as more appropriate for women than for men. Women are more likely to receive antidepressant medication; yet this rate actually exceeds the difference between women and men reporting depressive symptoms.

At the root of these differences lie processes that influence how men and women are perceived and diagnosed. These processes may account for the fact that twice as many women than men are diagnosed with depression, a conclusion reached by the American Psychological Association when it noted that higher levels of stress and abuse may account for the difference in rates of depression.

This *Web Investigation* concerns gender differences in the rates of a common psychological problem, depression. *To begin, go to the Morris Companion Web Site at the internet address above, select chapter 14, and click on* **Web Investigations**.

Multiple Choice Pretest

This pretest will help you identify the topics in the chapter that are most difficult for you. By focusing your study time in those areas, you will see the greatest improvement.

1. Insight therapies focus on giving people _____.
    a. skills to change their behaviors
    b. a better awareness of their feelings, motives, an actions
    c. an understanding of perceptual processes
    d. an understanding of biological influences on behavior

2. Which of the following is NOT a type of insight therapy?
    a. client-centered therapy
    b. psycholanalysis
    c. Gestalt therapy
    d. cognitive therapy

3. _____ is a technique in psychoanalysis where the patient lets his thoughts flow without interruption or inhibition.
    a. Positive transference
    b. Regression
    c. Free association
    d. Catharsis

4. A very important component of client-centered therapy is for the therapist to express _____ for the patient.
    a. psychological congruence
    b. unconditional positive regard
    c. positive transference
    d. conditional positive regard

5. The core principle behind _____ therapy is help clients help themselves to become fully functioning people.
    a. behavior therapy
    b. psychoanalysis
    c. gestalt therapy
    d. client-centered therapy

6. In Gestalt therapy, the therapist is _____ and _____.
    a. active; directive
    b. passive; nondirective
    c. passive; directive
    d. active; nondirective

7. The main focus of Gestalt therapy is _____
    a. early childhood influences on adult behavior
    b. the here-and-now
    c. finding the initial causes of current problems
    d. the role of early dysfunctional relationships in the development of problems

8. A recent study found that _____ of patients showed improvements after only eight therapy sessions.
    a. 25 percent
    b. 50 percent
    c. 75 percent
    d. 100 percent

9. The focus of behavioral therapist is to _____.
    a. get the patient to look past the problem
    b. provide a warm atmosphere for discussing problems
    c. teach a client more satisfying ways of behaving
    d. provide insight into the causes of the problem

10. The technique of _____ trains a client to remain relaxed and calm in the presence of a stimulus which he or she formerly feared.
    a. reciprocal inhibition
    b. free association
    c. systematic desensitization
    d. operant conditioning

11. What therapy uses real physical pain to change behavior?
    a. aversive conditioning
    b. psychoanalysis
    c. desensitization
    d. operant conditioning

12. What therapy uses reinforcement to change behavior?
    a. aversive conditioning
    b. psychoanalysis
    c. desensitization
    d. operant conditioning

13. A therapist believes that her client suffers from misconceptions about himself and his relationship to this environment based on unrealistic expectations of himself. The focus of therapy is to change the client's beliefs into more rational ones. The therapist probably is using _____ therapy techniques.
    a. client-centered
    b. rational-emotive
    c. psychoanalytic
    d. Gestalt

14. Which of the following is an advantage of group therapy?
    a. the client has the experience of interacting with other people in a therapeutic setting
    b. it often reveals a client's problems more quickly than individual therapy
    c. it can be cheaper than individual therapy
    d. all of the above

15. Smith and Glass (1977) reported that a client receiving therapy is better off than _____ percent of untreated control subjects.
    a. 25 percent
    b. 50 percent
    c. 75 percent
    d. 100 percent

16. There is a trend among psychotherapists to combine treatment techniques in what is called
_____.
    a. eclecticism
    b. humanistic therapy
    c. group treatment
    d. behavior therapy

17. Only _____ are licensed to give drug therapy.
    a. counselors
    b. psychologists
    c. psychiatrists
    d. therapists

Answers to Multiple Choice Pretest

1.   b.   Insight therapies focus on increasing awareness of feelings, motives and actions.

2.   d.   Cognitive therapy is not a type of insight therapy.

3.   c.   Free association involves freely reporting on one's thoughts without inhibition.

4.   b.   Client-centered therapists strive to express unconditional positive regard toward their clients.

5.   d.   Client-centered therapy seeks to help clients become fully functioning people.

6.   a.   Gestalt therapists are quite active and directive in therapy sessions.

7.   b.   The main focus of gestalt therapy is the "here-and-now".

8.   b.   About 50% of patients show improvement after only 8 therapy sessions.

9.   c.   Behavior therapy strives to teach clients to develop more satisfying ways of behaving.

10.   c.   Systematic desensitization trains clients to relax in the presence of fearful stimuli.

11.   a.   Aversive conditioning uses real, physical pain to change behavior.

12.   d.   Reinforcement is used by behavior therapists to change behavior.

13.   b.   Rational-emotive therapists seek to change irrational thoughts and behaviors

14.   d.   Groups afford all the benefits listed in the first three options.

15.   c.   On average someone in therapy is better off than about 75% of persons with comparable issues who are not in therapy.

16.   a.   Eclecticism refers to combining approaches.

17.   c.   Of the professions listed, only psychiatrists can prescribe medication.

Learning Objectives

After you have read and studied this chapter, you should be able to complete the following statements. Your exam is likely to be written based on these learning objectives.

1. Differentiate between insight therapies, behavior therapies, cognitive therapies, and group therapies.

2. Discuss the criticisms of psychoanalysis.

3. Explain how client-centered and rational-emotive therapists interpret causes of emotional problems. Describe the therapeutic techniques of each approach.

4. Summarize the behavioral therapist's interpretation of disorders. Describe aversive conditioning, desensitization, and modeling.

5. Describe stress-inoculation therapy, Beck's cognitive therapy, and Gestalt therapy.

6. List the advantages and disadvantages of group therapies. Identify five current approaches to group therapy.

7. Discuss the effectiveness of insight therapy and behavior therapy.

8. Outline the available biological treatments and discuss the advantages and disadvantages of each.

9. Summarize the inadequacies of institutionalization. List the alternative to institutionalization.

10. Explain the differences between primary, secondary, and tertiary prevention.

11. Discuss possible areas of misunderstanding when there are cultural differences in therapy.

Short Essay Questions

Write out your answers to the following four essay questions to further your mastery of the topics.

1.   Are biological treatments like psychosurgery and ECT ever justified?   Explain.

_____

_____

_____

_____

_____

_____

_____

_____

_____

_____

_____

2.   Summarize the research on the effectiveness of various types of psychotherapy.

_____

_____

_____

_____

_____

_____

_____

_____

_____

3.   Describe the advantages and goals of group therapy.   Identify two types of group therapy.

_____

_____

_____

_____

_____

_____

_____

_____

_____

_____

_____

4.   Outline the steps involved in systematic desensitization. Give an example.

_____

_____

_____

_____

_____

_____

_____

_____

_____

_____

_____

_____

5. Compare behavior therapy with insight-oriented therapy. Give examples.

_____

_____

_____

_____

_____

_____

_____

_____

_____

_____

_____

_____

6. Discuss gender and cultural differences in the effectiveness of various types of therapy.

_____

_____

_____

_____

_____

_____

_____

_____

_____

Language Support

Students identified the following words from the text as needing more explanation. This page can be cut out, folded in half, and used as a bookmark for this chapter.

A

abstinence	do not do the behavior
accurate	true
adage	saying
advent	beginning
alleviating	get rid of
ambulatory	people are able to walk
awkwardness	feeling uneasy or uncomfortable

C

cardinal rule	most important rule
clam up	stop talking
coarsening	getting rougher and not as nice
commonsense	logical; understandable to many people
constrained	held back

D

defensiveness	protecting yourself
derogatory	negative
dysfunctional	cause problems for you

E

edgewise	in between
emphatically	very strongly
enhancing	increasing
enviable	something others want
establishment	starting
exemplify	show

extent	amount

F

fantasies	thoughts about imaginary things
fraught with	troubled by

H

hodgepodge	confusing mixture

I

impassive	not willing to change
inconsistent	does not stay the same
inhibiting	stopping, preventing
innermost	private thoughts

L

lethargy	very tired; without energy
lurk	stay hidden

M

makeshift	thrown together quickly and not carefully
manifest	seen
mere	only

N

neutrality	not favoring one side or the other

O

overbearing	too strong and controlling
orthodox	traditional

P

prognosis	likely future changes in the disorder (problem)
proliferation	growth; large increase

R

restore	get back

revelations	explanations that tell new information
rigidity	stiffness

S

self-perpetuating	tends to continue by itself
simultaneously	at the same time
social stigma	looked down on by other people
spiral	spread out into
stroke	pet

T

tarantula	very large spider
testify	to make a strong statement
transition	change
treatment modality	way of treating

U

underfunded	not enough money
underscores	emphasizes

V

vehemently	very strongly
vigorously	strongly, with much effort
vulnerable	weak, open to dangers

W

warehouses for victims	large buildings in which people with mental disorders live
wariness	fearfulness

Multiple Choice Posttest

After studying the text and completing the Study Guide activities, answer these questions to determine if you need to review any areas before the course exam.

1. Often the techniques used by therapists today utilize_____.
   a. the humanistic approach
   b. the psychoanalytic approach
   c. the behavioral approach
   d. not just one approach

2. The recent trend toward short-term psychodynamic psychotherapy has resulted in _____.
   a. focusing more on the client's current life situation and relationships
   b. a dramatic decline in effectiveness of psychotherapy
   c. a greater reliance on psychiatric interventions
   d. therapists becoming more neutral and "hands-off" with their clients

3. All of the following are disadvantages of traditional psychoanalysis, except:
   a. the patient must be highly motivated to change and to deal rationally with whatever the analysis uncovers
   b. analysis may take five years or longer
   c. analysis is effective only with severely disturbed patients
   d. it does not give immediate help for immediate problems

4. Insight therapies focus on giving people _____.
   a. skills to change their behaviors
   b. clearer understanding of their feelings, motives, an actions
   c. an understanding of perceptual processes
   d. an understanding of biological influences on behavior

5. All of the following are insight therapies EXCEPT _____.
   a. client-centered therapy
   b. psychoanalysis
   c. Gestalt therapy
   d. cognitive therapy

6. _____ is a very important component of client-centered therapy.
   a. Psychological congruence
   b. Conditional positive regard
   c. Positive transference
   d. Unconditional positive regard

7. Gestalt therapy is most concerned with _____.
   a. early childhood influences on adult behavior
   b. responding authentically to the present moment and situation
   c. finding the initial causes of current problems
   d. the role of early dysfunctional relationships in the development of problems

8. Behavior therapists seek to _____.
   a. get patient to look past their problems
   b. provide a warm atmosphere for discussing problems
   c. help change clients' behaviors in positive ways
   d. provide insight into the causes of the problem

9. The technique of _____ trains a client to remain relaxed and calm in the presence of a stimulus which causes anxiety for him/her.
   a. reciprocal inhibition
   b. free association
   c. systematic desensitization
   d. operant conditioning

10. A therapist believes that her client suffers from irrational thoughts about himself and has unrealistic expectations of himself. The focus of therapy is to change the client's beliefs into more rational ones by challenging the irrational beliefs. The therapist probably is using _____ therapy techniques.
    a. client-centered
    b. rational-emotive
    c. psychoanalytic
    d. Gestalt

11. All of the following are advantages of groups relative to individual therapy sessions, except:
    a. Group therapy is less expensive for each participant
    b. Groups offer social support
    c. Groups can help people to learn useful new
    d. Anxiety and self-critical orientations are masked in group settings

12. _____ are mental-health practitioners who are licensed to give medication.
    a. Counselors
    b. Psychologists
    c. Psychiatrists
    d. Therapists

13. Most antipsychotic drugs work by _____.
    a. increasing acetylcholine in the brain
    b. increasing serotonin in the brain
    c. inhibiting the function of the hypothalamus
    d. blocking dopamine receptors in the brain

14. "Prozac" is a medication used for _____.
    a. hallucinations
    b. depression
    c. mania
    d. psychosurgery

15. The effects of psychosurgery _____.
    a. do not include undesirable side effects
    b. are useless in controlling pain
    c. are all negative
    d. are difficult to predict

16. Electroconvulsive therapy is considered _____ effective in treating _____ cases of depression.
    a. highly; mild
    b. highly; severe
    c. slightly ; mild
    d. slightly; severe

17. Which of the following treatments is LEAST likely to be used today?
    a. electroconvulsive therapy
    b. drug treatment
    c. prefrontal lobotomy
    d. shock therapy

18. The focus of _____ prevention is intervention.
    a. basic
    b. primary
    c. secondary
    d. tertiary

19. In Native American culture, not making eye contact and looking downward during a conversation is a sign of _____.
    a. respect
    b. denigration
    c. appreciation
    d. depression

20. Alcoholics Anonymous is an example of a _____.
    a. psychoanalytic therapy group
    b. self-help group
    c. desensitization group
    d. structured behavior therapy group

Answers to Multiple Choice Posttest

1.   d.   Most therapists today are eclectic in their approach to treatment.

2.   a.   Short-term therapy tends to focus on current problems and life situations of clients.

3.   c.   Psychoanalysis is not effective with severely disturbed clients.

4.   b.   Insight therapies focus on promoting clearer understanding of feelings, motives and behaviors in clients.

5.   d.   Cognitive therapy is not an insight therapy

6.   d.   Client-centered therapy relies much on the provision of unconditional positive regard by the therapist toward the client.

7.   b.   Gestalt therapists strive to teach clients to respond to the present moment and situation.

8.   c.   Behavior therapists seek to help clients to make positive behavior changes.

9.   c.   Systematic desensitization involves working through an anxiety hierarchy.

10.   b.   Rational-emotive therapists challenge irrational thoughts.

11.   d.   Group settings tend to bring out such maladaptive tendencies.

12.   c.   Psychiatrists are licensed to prescribe medication.

13.   d.   Anti-psychotic medications work by blocking dopamine receptors in the brain.

14.   b.   Prozac is a commonly prescribed medication for depression.

15.   d.   It is difficult to predict the effects of psychosurgery.

16.   b.   ECT often works well for cases of severe depression.

17.   c.   Prefrontal lobotomies are not used today.

18.   c.   Secondary prevention entails intervention.

19.   a.   Respect is transmitted by avoiding eye contact in Native American cultures.

20.   b.   AA is an example of a self-help group.

15

Social Psychology

Class and Text Notes

Social psychology is the scientific study of the ways in which the thoughts, feelings, and behaviors of one individual are influenced by the real, imagined, or inferred behavior or characteristics of other people.

1. Social Cognition

    A. Impression Formation

        • Schemata

            - Primacy effect

            - Self-fulfilling prophecy

        • Stereotypes

Enduring Issues: Interpreting Behavior

    B. Attribution

        • Explaining behavior

        • Biases in attributions

            - Fundamental attribution error

            - Defensive attribution

            - Just-world hypothesis

        • Attribution across cultures

    C. Interpersonal Attraction

        • Proximity

        • Physical attractiveness

        • Similarity

        • Exchange

        • Intimacy

Thinking Critically: Intimacy and the Internet

2.   Attitudes

    A.   The Nature of Attitudes

        • Attitudes and behaviors

            - Self-monitoring

        • Attitude development

    B.   Prejudice and Discrimination

Enduring Issues: Does Discrimination Reflect Prejudice?

        • Prejudice

        • Sources of prejudice

            - Frustration-aggression theory

            - Authoritarian personality

            - Racism

        • Strategies for Reducing Prejudice and Discrimination

Applying Psychology: Understanding Ethnic Conflict and Violence

    C.   Attitude Change

        • The process of persuasion

        • The communication model

        • Cognitive dissonance theory

Thinking Critically: Attitudes Toward Smoking

3.   Social Influence

    A.   Cultural Influence

        • Cultural truism

        • Norm

    B.   Cultural Assimilators

    C.   Conformity

        • Conformity across cultures

Enduring Issues: Social Influence Across Cultures

    D.   Compliance

Web Investigations
www.prenhall.com/morris

Chapter 15: Predicting Our Own Social Behavior

After reading this chapter, you probably have the sense that most people are sensitive to the behavior of others. We watch others to discern the causes of their actions, to learn more about the situation in which they act, and to suggest to us how we might or should behave ourselves. These observations are stimulated by more than mere curiosity. Other people influence us—and we them—through leadership, demands for obedience, requests for compliance, and the sometimes-subtle changes that happen through conformity. Poet John Donne (1572-1631) noted the interdependent nature of people and their influences when he penned, "No man is an Island, entire of itself; every man is a piece of the Continent, a part of the main. (*Meditation XVII*)."

We spend all of our lives influencing and being influenced by others, so we have ample experience with the behavior of others. But we have even more experience with our own actions. Our knowledge of what we would do should help us to predict what others would do as well. This *Web Investigation* is intended to provide insight into our own behavior and the reasons why social psychologists sometime construct elaborate studies that will illuminate the causes of our actions.

To begin, go to the Morris Companion Web Site at the internet address shown above, select chapter 15, and click on **Web Investigations.** Gain insights about yourself as you learn more about the social world.

Multiple Choice Pretest

This pretest will help you identify the topics in the chapter that are most difficult for you. By focusing your study time in those areas, you will see the greatest improvement.

1. The study of the way thoughts, feelings and behaviors of a person are affected by the perceived characteristics of others is known as _____ psychology.
    a. interpersonal
    b. social
    c. environmental
    d. cognitive

2. The _____ effect occurs when our first impressions influence our opinion about someone more than current information.
    a. halo
    b. recency
    c. primacy
    d. phi phenomenon

3. When the expectation of one person influences the behavior of another person, the expectation has become a(n) _____.
    a. response characteristic
    b. primary drive
    c. attribution
    d. self-fulfilling prophecy

4. A(n) _____ is the belief that all members of a social category have the same characteristics.
    a. perception
    b. primacy effect
    c. stereotype
    d. unifying trait

5. According to Heider, we usually attribute someone's behavior to _____.
    a. internal and external causes at the same time
    b. either internal or external causes, but not both at the same time
    c. external causes only
    d. internal causes only

6. According to Jones and Nisbett, we tend to attribute our own actions to _____ factors and the behavior of others to _____ factors.
    a. situational; personal
    b. situational; situational
    c. personal; personal
    d. personal; situational

7. The _____ is when we place too much emphasis on personal factors when trying to explain other people's actions.
    a. Peter principle
    b. primacy effect
    c. fundamental attribution error
    d. defensive attribution

8. The most important factor in interpersonal attraction is _____.
   a. reciprocity
   b. attractiveness
   c. similarity
   d. proximity

9. Being attracted to someone because of opposite interests or personality characteristics is called _____.
   a. reciprocity
   b. complementarity
   c. rewardingness
   d. proximity

10. Liking someone who has expressed a liking for us is called _____.
    a. exchange
    b. proximity
    c. reciprocity
    d. complementarity

11. _____ is a very important part of intimate communication.
    a. Kinesics
    b. Self-disclosure
    c. Deindividuation
    d. Proxemics

12. When a person observes a situation for cues about how to react, this is called _____.
    a. situational narcissism
    b. self-efficacy
    c. reaction formation
    d. self-monitoring

13. Prejudice is to a(n) _____ as discrimination is to a(n) _____.
    a. unfavorable attitude; unfair act
    b. tolerance; oppression
    c. unfair act; unfavorable attitude
    d. oppression; tolerance

14. People who are punished for problems they did not cause are called _____.
    a. bigots
    b. victims
    c. scapegoats
    d. egalitarian

15. The message which MOST likely will result in a change of attitude is a message with _____.
    a. high fear from a highly credible source
    b. high fear from a moderately credible source
    c. moderate fear from a highly credible source
    d. moderate fear from a moderately credible source

16. When trying to change someone's opinion, it is generally better to _____.
    a. present only your side of an argument
    b. present only criticisms of the opposing viewpoint
    c. present both sides of an argument, giving the opposing side first
    d. present both sides of an argument, giving your side first

17. The most powerful method of changing people's opinions is usually _____.
    a. a media presentation
    b. "word of mouth"
    c. personal contact
    d. a written argument

18. People with _____ are more easily influenced to change their attitudes.
    a. low self-esteem
    b. high self-esteem
    c. low achievement need
    d. high achievement need

19. The bystander effect is the tendency for:
    a. people to help out when they see a need
    b. the likelihood of help occurring lessening as more people are present
    c. the seriousness of an emergency to be misperceived by bystanders
    d. people who witness an emergency to help only if they are similar to the victim

Answers to Multiple Choice Pretest

1. b.   Social psychology studies how people's thoughts, feelings, and behaviors are affected by perceived characteristics of others.

2. c.   The primacy effect entails how our first impressions affect our later thoughts and behaviors.

3. d.   Self-fulfilling prophecy is the influence of one's expectations about others on those others.

4. c.   Believing that all members of a group have the same characteristics is stereotyping.

5. b.   Attributions can be either internal or external.

6. a.   We tend to attribute our own behaviors to situational factors and others' to personal factors.

7. c.   Placing too much weight on personal factors when explaining others' behavior is called the fundamental attribution error.

8. d.   Proximity is the most important factor in interpersonal attraction.

9. b.   Attraction between "opposites" is referred to as complementarity.

10. a.   Exchange involves liking someone who expressed liking for us.

11. b.   Self-disclosure is a key factor for progressive deepening of intimate communication.

12. d.   Self-monitoring entails observing a situation for cues about how to react.

13. a.   Prejudice is an attitude; discrimination is an action.

14. c.   Scapegoats are punished for problems they did not cause.

15. c.   The greatest amount of attitude change comes when a highly credible source instills a moderate amount of fear in the audience.

16. d.   A balance approach is best, especially if you present your views first.

17. c.   Personal contact is usually the most powerful way of changing people's opinions.

18. a.   Low self-esteem is associated with greater likelihood of attitude change.

19. b.   As the number of bystanders increases, the chances of one of them helping decreases.

Learning Objectives

After you have read and studied this chapter, you should be able to complete the following statements. Your exam is likely to emphasize these learning objectives.

1. Describe the process by which we form first impressions of other people. Identify three factors that influence personal perception.

2. Explain three aspects of attribution and explain attribution errors.

3. Explain the dynamics of interpersonal attraction.

4. Identify the components of attitudes. Discuss the relationship between attitude and behavior.

5. Explain how attitudes are formed and changed.

6. Explain the origin of prejudice and discrimination and how prejudice can be reduced.

7. Discuss the dynamics of attitude change and the process of persuasion.

8. Explain the theory of cognitive dissonance. List some ways to reduce cognitive dissonance.

9. Define risky shift and polarization. Summarize the conditions under which groups are effective and ineffective in solving problems.

10. Explain how culture, conformity, compliance, and obedience exert social influence.

11. Identify the four types of social action.

12. Discuss the theories of leadership.

Short Essay Questions

Write out your answers to the following four essay questions to further your mastery of the topics.

1. Does the norm of obedience to an authority figure alter an individual's responsibility for his or her behavior? Explain.

_____

_____

_____

_____

_____

_____

_____

_____

_____

_____

_____

2. Identify and describe the factors that influence the formation of impressions about people.

_____

_____

_____

_____

_____

_____

_____

_____

_____

_____

_____

3. Identify five factors that influence the effectiveness of efforts to change people's attitudes.

_____

_____

_____

_____

_____

_____

_____

_____

_____

_____

4. Describe the factors influencing group decision making and the effectiveness of groups.

_____

_____

_____

_____

_____

_____

_____

_____

_____

_____

5. Do opposites attract? Explain.

_____

_____

_____

_____

_____

_____

_____

_____

_____

_____

6. Differentiate among the following: prejudice, stereotype, discrimination, racism. Give examples.

_____

_____

_____

_____

_____

_____

_____

_____

_____

_____

_____

7.   Describe some factors that affect group decision making. Give examples.

_____

_____

_____

_____

_____

_____

_____

_____

_____

_____

8.   List some factors that impact the decision to intervene in an emergency. Give examples.

_____

_____

_____

_____

_____

_____

_____

_____

_____

_____

Language Support

Students identified the following words from the text as needing more explanation. This page can be cut out, folded in half, and used as a bookmark for this chapter.

A

acquiesce	approve of, say yes to
albeit	however, but
amiability	get along
animated	actions were full of energy
arouse	to bring up

B

beyond	further
blatant	obvious, easy to see

C

candor	openness
cognitive dissonance	thinking something is not right
cohesiveness	working together well
comply	go along with
comprehend	understand
conform	go along with
consensus	everyone agrees
contradictory	do not agree
counterarguments	statements against
convictions	beliefs

D

demonstrable	can be shown
depicted	shown
discrepant	not compatible

E

emerged	came out
endorsements	supporting statements
exerting	trying hard

G

genuine	real
governed	controlled

H

harbored	hid, concealed

I

indecisive	cannot make a decision
inducement	bribe, payment
inevitably	will certainly happen

L

loathing	to hate a lot
lure	tempt, make us do something we normally would not do

M

menacing	frightening, scary
mystification	mystery around it

O

optimism	thinking good things will happen

P

perpetuating	making something last
persisted	lasted
persuasive	convincing
pervasive	general, all over
presume	believe something is right even without a good reason
propel	lead to

Q

quota   a certain amount that is supposed to be reached

R

rationalization   excuse

repetitive tasks   things done over and over again

S

salient   main, most important

scanty   too little

scarcely   very little

scare tactics   something designed to frighten us

seize   grab suddenly

simplistic   simple

speculation   guesses

steeped   full of

straightforward   obvious, direct

subtly   not obvious, secretly

T

transcend   go above, not to consider

U

unforeseen   not aware of before

V

vent   release

Multiple Choice Posttest

After studying the text and completing the Study Guide activities, answer these questions to determine if you need to review any areas before the course exam.

1. A behavioral rule shared by a whole society is called a _____.
    a. cultural more
    b. folkway
    c. cultural truism
    d. cultural norm

2. Laws are typically based on _____.
    a. cultural more
    b. folkway
    c. cultural truism
    d. cultural norm

3. All of the following are likely to increase an individual's conformity to group behavior EXCEPT
    a. the person is attracted to the group.
    b. the person expects to interact with the - group.
    c. the person feels accepted by the group.
    d. the person is of relatively low status in the group.

4. The _____ effect is that people are more likely to comply with a second, larger request after complying with a first, small request.
    a. response cue
    b. bait and switch
    c. foot-in-the-door
    d. primacy

5. _____ is a process by which people feel anonymous in a large group.
    a. Deindividuation
    b. Identity diffusion
    c. Identity moratorium
    d. Social facilitation

6. In a mob, one dominant person can often convince people to act due to the _____ effect.
    a. lowball
    b. snowball
    c. primacy
    d. door-in-the-face

7. _____ behavior is helping other people with no expectation of personal gain.
    a. Reciprocal
    b. Deindividuated
    c. Diffused
    d. Altruistic

8. When there is so much pressure from the group to conform that people do not feel free to express critical ideas, this is called _____.
    a. groupthink
    b. polarization
    c. risky shift
    d. deindividuation

9. The poor decisions made in the Watergate cover-up, the Challenger disaster and the Bay of Pigs invasion were due primarily to _____.
   a. groupthink
   b. polarization
   c. risky shift
   d. deindividuation

10. The focus of industrial/organizational psychology is _____.
   a. strategies for founding an economically successful business
   b. behavior in organizational settings
   c. the effects of industrialization on the environment
   d. personal problems of employed people

11. In the Mayo study of workers at the Hawthorne plant, _____.
   a. productivity improved as lighting was decreased
   b. productivity improved as lighting was increased
   c. productivity improved no matter what was done to the lighting conditions
   d. none of the above

12. Which of the following did Rempel and Holmes NOT recommend for developing and strengthening trust?
   a. focus on specific actions rather than motives
   b. focus on how to improve the person
   c. don't dwell on negative memories
   d. be fair and realistic in interpreting someone's behavior

13. Someone who falls at work is MOST likely to attribute the fall to _____.
   a. problems he is having in his personal life
   b. errors in judgment on his part
   c. a slick surface at work
   d. being distracted by thoughts about the weekend

14. The term psychologists use for how close two people live to each other is _____.
   a. propinquity
   b. proximity
   c. reciprocity
   d. complementarily

15. Rebecca consistently expresses her beliefs with little regard for the constraints imposed by the situation. She is probably a _____ self-monitor.
   a. reactive
   b. nonreactive
   c. low
   d. high

16. Which of the following personality types is MOST likely to be prejudiced?
   a. altruistic
   b. egalitarian
   c. authoritarian
   d. intellectual

17. Reducing racial prejudice can be best accomplished by _____.
   a. education
   b. contact
   c. competition
   d. cooperation

Answers to Multiple Choice Posttest

1. d.   Cultural norms are behavioral rules shared by a whole society.

2. d.   Laws are typically based on cultural norms.

3. c.   Feeling accepted by the group will not consistently promote conformity.

4. c.   The foot-in-the-door procedure increases compliance to a target request if it follows a small request.

5. a.   Deindividuation involves feeling anonymous in a large group.

6. b.   The snowball effect involves the effect of a dominant person on the actions of others in a group

7. d.   Altruism is helping others without expectation of personal gain.

8. a.   Groupthink is great pressure on group members to conform by not expressing critical ideas.

9. a.   Groupthink has resulted in many poor decisions on high stakes issues.

10. b.   Industrial/organizational psychologists study behavior in organizations.

11. c.   The Hawthorne effect entails people working harder merely because they are being watched.

12. b.   Trust can be strengthened by all strategies listed except improving the person.

13. c.   Such an accident is likely to produce an external attribution (e.g., the floor was slick).

14. b.   Proximity refers to closeness in terms of location.

15. c.   Low self-monitors are more likely to speak without considering the situation.

16. c.   Authoritarian personality types are most likely to be prejudiced.

17. d.   Cooperation is a very effective means for reducing prejudice.